Enchilada
Entrepreneur

*Ten Lessons in Life and Business
from the Founder of a Successful
Tex-Mex Restaurant Group*

RUSSELL YBARRA

RIVER GROVE
BOOKS

Published by River Grove Books
Austin, TX
www.rivergrovebooks.com

Distributed by River Grove Books

Design and composition by Greenleaf Book Group and Mimi Bark
Cover design by Greenleaf Book Group and Lauren Smith
Cover images used under license from ©iStock.com/ugurhan

Publisher's Cataloging-in-Publication data is available.

Print ISBN: 978-1-63299-810-1

eBook ISBN: 978-1-63299-811-8

First Edition

Foreword

~~~~~~

As I considered what I might have to offer by way of introducing this book, and its author, I noticed that I was overthinking it. Several days tolled, and I felt terrible about it. Three words popped into my mind: *sense of urgency*. Every time I've asked Russell Ybarra to contribute to a charitable cause, to mentor a small-business owner, or to speak at a school or organization, his reply, and action, has been immediate. Shockingly so. If he's sending a check for veterans with PTSD or children with cancer, he won't mail it; he'll drive it, such that it's in my hands within thirty minutes of calling to ask him. His office is perhaps more than that many minutes away. He will include a note: "sense of urgency." He doesn't procrastinate. He doesn't delay. He doesn't make me ask again. He engages. He gives a sense of urgency to something that isn't urgent to him, and then, just like that, it is. It's striking. Almost jarring. It humbles me. It makes me want to be more like that.

I think that's the story this book really tells. This isn't a book by Russell Ybarra of things you should do. It's a book of what he does and why he does those things, including candid confessions of failures from which he grew and that he doesn't shirk. Chapter 7's "sense of urgency" isn't advice so much as a description of how he lives. He does every one of these things, often to the exclusion of the easy path, the typical path.

On September 12, 1962, President John F. Kennedy spoke at Rice University in Houston, where Russell's cousin has been the dean of the Jesse H. Jones Graduate School of Business since 2016. He delivered a call to arms, not just for NASA to send a man to the moon but for all of us to soar beyond the outer space of our own limiting barriers and fears:

> We choose to go to the moon. We choose to go to the moon in this decade and do the other things, not because they are easy, but because they are hard, because that goal will serve to organize and measure the best of our energies and skills, because that challenge is one that we are willing to accept, one we are unwilling to postpone, and one which we intend to win, and the others, too.[1]

---

1   John F. Kennedy, "We Choose to Go to the Moon," speech delivered at Rice University, Houston, TX, September 12, 1962, https://www.rice.edu/jfk-speech.

This book isn't really a "how to"; it's a "why not?" It doesn't lecture or brag but, rather, challenges each of us to demand more of ourselves and not to wait. It challenges each of us to use our business, our treasure, and our skills to help others, because in doing so, there is a rewarding joy.

Reading this book was not so much learning but confirming for me. I've seen the way Russell Ybarra lives his life. It's exactly what he lays out here.

I hope you enjoy reading this book as much as I've enjoyed being Russell's friend. He likes to call himself the Master Enchilada Roller, a way of humbling himself as the frontline worker, the infantryman, the common man, the unpretentious one. I like that. It should be noted, though, that in his life, the most important thing he's ever made has not been enchiladas. He's made a difference.

MICHAEL BERRY
Czar of Talk

Open for Business

~~~~~~

At 11:00 a.m. on January 11, 1993, I pulled the string on the neon "open" sign in the window of my new restaurant for the very first time. Gringo's Tex-Mex was officially in business.

Truth be told, I didn't want to open that restaurant. Up until that point in my life, I had failed at almost everything I had attempted. I had failed at selling sports cars. I had failed at selling satellite dishes. I had even failed at sustaining a Mexican restaurant I opened in 1989. Now, I was about to start a business in the same location where four previous ones had failed, including a Mexican restaurant run by my family. Opening this restaurant would probably be the next failure in my life. But I felt I had nothing else to fall back on.

That morning, as I waited for the first customer to arrive, I couldn't imagine that thirty-one years later, not only would the original location still be going strong, but I would also have fifteen more Gringo's locations—plus another restaurant chain, Jimmy Changas—around the Houston metropolitan area. I would become known in the community as the Master Enchilada Roller.

All this from a kid who barely made it out of high school.

I was a terrible student in school, and college was not even a consideration. I grew up in a restaurant family. My father owned El Toro Restaurants, based in Baytown, Texas, east of Houston. My mother practically raised me, my six brothers, and my one sister alone because my dad was so busy working all the time. Inevitably, I spent time working in my father's restaurants throughout my childhood—dishwasher, food preparation, line cook, and so on.

In fact, that's where I learned to roll enchiladas. When I was fifteen, a cousin stopped by when I was working in one of the El Toro kitchens, and he began to make himself some enchiladas. I noticed he was putting them together incorrectly, trying to soften crispy taco shells instead of using soft corn tortillas in the first place. At that moment, I realized that by working as a line cook every day after school, I had actually learned how to roll an enchilada the right way!

That day began my quest to master rolling enchiladas. Today, it reminds me to be a Master Enchilada Roller in all I do.

But during my teens and into my twenties, I couldn't imagine a path to success for myself. I lacked self-confidence because I did not go to college, and I felt I did not have a specific skill set that would make me appealing enough to be hired by a company other than a restaurant. I knew that if I were going to be successful, I would have to figure it out for myself, but I just didn't have any clue how or where to begin.

Then came that string of business failures. I thought a business's primary goal was to make money—and as much of it as possible. But I discontinued that belief quickly after I experienced so many failures that failure itself started to feel way too normal. Any thoughts I had about how a company becomes successful had to be thrown out the window, and I needed to start the process over from scratch. Little did I realize at the time, but those failures were actually my best teachers in disguise. I had learned what not to do, so I began looking for successful companies that I could observe and learn from—and I slowly began to develop my habits of success.

One major hurdle for me was that lack of self-confidence. But I received a major revelation during the mid-1980s while working at the El Toro in La Porte, a suburb east of Houston. I attended a luncheon hosted by the local chamber of commerce, and the company they hired to cater the event did such a fantastic job that it caught my attention. I made my way over to the buffet line and started a conversation with the catering company's owner.

After she learned that I worked in the restaurant industry, she asked me if our company also offered catering. I don't remember exactly what I said or how I must have said it, but I do remember that this woman stopped me mid-sentence and said, "Well, if you don't believe in yourself, no one else will!"

It was like she took a huge piece of lumber and hit me upside the head with it. She was absolutely correct. If I did not believe in myself, if I lacked confidence in my ability to do anything worthwhile, then how in the world was I ever going to get anyone else to believe in me?

Still, it's hard to get past years of frustration and failure. When I decided to open the first Gringo's in that location where other restaurants had failed, I felt like I had no other choice. My family still owned the property after several attempts to sell it and owed the monthly mortgage payment. I don't know why, but I remember the amount—$4,852.10. It was a difficult payment at the time, especially since the building was just sitting there empty.

However, in opening the first Gringo's on that spot, I made one important decision that would make a difference in my failure rate. I had decided to no longer focus on making money—yes, you read that right! Instead, I would focus on making the very best product I knew how to make, and I would offer it at the best possible price.

Today, we employ 2,600 team members and serve thousands of meals each week across our portfolio of restaurants—Gringo's, Jimmy Changas, Burger Libre, and the Lunch Box. Back in school, I certainly would not have been voted "most likely to succeed," but through perseverance and paying close attention to others' habits of success, I developed a formula built on my habits.

THE FORMULA FOR SUCCESS

This book details ten habits that have contributed to my success as the Master Enchilada Roller. But where do habits come from? Values.

When we do what we value, we value what we do. Values are the result of what you truly believe, and your core values are the ones that are nonnegotiable.

Along the way, our company developed five core values that drive everything we do. Values create habits, and habits lead to success or failure. When you have positive, constructive values that you hold in esteem and communicate to your team members and customers, you have the formula for success.

Positive values = Positive habits = Success

The five core values at Gringo's are:

1. Building guest relationships one meal at a time
2. Fostering honesty and respect among our team members
3. Reinvesting in our team members and local community
4. Developing a relationship of trust with our vendors
5. Never being satisfied

WHY I WROTE THIS BOOK

I wrote this book for several reasons. First, I want my grandchildren to know who their papa was, other than an older man who liked to show them the magic tricks he learned on YouTube.

Second, I want to show my respect and support for U.S. military service members and veterans. I will donate the proceeds from this book to an organization for which I'm a longtime supporter—the Houston-based nonprofit organization PTSD Foundation of America. This peer-to-peer resident program helps veterans deal with the unseen wounds of war.

Third, I want to write about my life to encourage parents not to lose faith in their children should they not measure up to the world's expectations of what it means to be educated. Knowledge encompasses a broad spectrum and can be found everywhere besides a college classroom.

Finally, I want Gringo's Tex-Mex and its business lessons to live long past my expiration date here on Earth. I recently turned sixty-two, and as another restaurant owner of similar age told me a few months ago, "Russell, I'm living in the last quarter of my life. Anything past eighty years old is overtime."

I hope to make it way past eighty years on this earth, but that statement really makes me think about how fast life goes by. The culture that my leadership team and I have established at Gringo's is way too precious just to let slip away because its founder is no longer around.

My hope is that this book will supply future team members and other young entrepreneurs with some of the habits of success

I learned and developed along the way, habits that have helped create the amazing company we are today.

While I've learned many lessons over the years, I hope the ten success habits in this book will help you commit to making the right choices in your life and work. I know that when you do that, you can have the life and business you desire.

Here's a quick list of my ten habits of success. Consider each one a dish from the kitchen of success. We dive deeper into one success habit per chapter.

1. *Do more than what you're paid for.* It's one of the easiest ways to get noticed in a crowded field.

2. *Always look for ways to improve.* Absolute perfection can never be achieved, but that should not stop you from trying.

3. *Guard your reputation.* It's the most valuable asset you will ever possess.

4. *Develop the habit of giving.* Give, and it will be given back to you.

5. *Surround yourself with people who make you better.* "Iron sharpens iron, and one man sharpens another."[2]

6. *Don't let fear of failure paralyze you.* Within every failure is a seed of equivalent success.

---

2   Proverbs 27:17 (English Standard Version).

7. *Develop a sense of urgency.* Without a sense of urgency, desire loses its value.

8. *Take responsibility for your actions.* Don't blame others for your situation.

9. *Live way below your means.* Don't spend money you don't possess to buy things you don't need to impress people you don't like.

10. *Live by the Golden Rule.* Everything you do to and for another person, you do to and for yourself.

CHAPTER 1

Do More than What You're Paid For

~~~~~~

The two most important words I ever wrote were
on that first Wal-Mart sign: "Satisfaction Guaranteed."
They're still up there, and they have made all
the difference.

—**SAM WALTON,** *Made in America*

"How can I give more than is expected of me?" I encourage
you to spend some time each day asking this question.
Then apply the answer: Plant service and harvest money.

Acquiring money to support one's lifestyle is a constant focus
for almost all of us. It is the reason for so much of our effort

and certainly the main goal of any success-oriented person. But most people use a completely backward approach when they try to make money.

Everywhere you see people with a money-first attitude, you usually see people who don't have very much of it. Or they are negatively affected because they care more about money than anything else.

Why?

People with a money-first attitude become so money-conscious that they forget that money cannot be harvested unless you plant the seeds that grow money. That happened to me before I realized that, to achieve success, I needed to focus not solely on making money but rather on how to best serve my customers.

Because the seed of money is service toward others, a "service-first attitude" is so important to grow money. It is what has the potential to create wealth. Put service first, and the rest takes care of itself.

The servers who concentrate on giving the best possible service combined with hospitality, making their customers feel welcome, don't need to worry about their tips; they will get plenty of them. But those servers who check on their tips throughout their shift won't find much in the way of gratuities because their focus is backward.

The line cook who focuses on building the picture-perfect plate will do fine on future paychecks. But the line cook who says, "Why should I put out extra effort for what they're paying me?" will be stuck with the same pay rate for a long time to come.

Here is a simple yet powerful rule to help you develop a service-first attitude: Each little something extra you do for others is a money seed. Volunteering to work an extra shift is a money seed. Giving guests extra service is a money seed because it brings those guests back. You may not see the rewards immediately, but if you're patient, those money seeds will grow to maturity and pay out in the end.

BUILDING A SERVICE-FIRST AND VALUE-FIRST CULTURE

I enjoy studying companies that are leaders in their particular industries. When it comes to service-first business cultures, one of the companies I immediately think of is the major convenience store chain Buc-ee's. Headquartered just south of Houston in Lake Jackson, Texas, Buc-ee's has risen to the top of the pack in its industry because it recognizes and delivers on two basic fundamentals—clean restrooms and fast checkout service.

This sounds simple enough, but think about this—when was the last time you went into a clean gas station restroom?

Buc-ee's models a service-first culture by going above and beyond to ensure all visitors get the same clean and efficient experience. Considering the company's expanding list of stores, their method seems to work.

My goal is for Gringo's to do for Tex-Mex restaurants what Buc-ee's does for convenience stores. While the moving parts are a little different in the restaurant business, I believe there are certain expectations diners have when eating out. They want great-tasting food at a fair price, they want efficient service, and they want the establishment to be clean.

While I'll be the first to admit we have come up short a few times in delivering a perfect experience, I'll also be the first to say that we'll do whatever it takes to make things right when given the opportunity. We aren't satisfied until our customers are.

We work hard to go above and beyond for our guests, both in how we treat them and in providing a great experience for a great value. For instance, I received a message recently from a guest complimenting our staff and our general manager, who helped her while she was picking up a to-go order. She said that a server and the general manager saw her waiting for her order and, despite being extremely busy, made an effort to walk over to her and say hello. The general manager even carried her order out to her car.

There's a huge difference between service and hospitality. Service is what the customer expects to receive; hospitality is all about how we make our customers feel while they're in our restaurant enjoying a delicious meal. It's about us taking the opportunity to express our gratitude for their patronage.

Most full-service casual Mexican restaurants provide complimentary tortilla chips and salsa to every table. At Gringo's, we go further by also providing our customers complimentary green sauce as well as soft-serve ice cream they serve themselves as they're leaving the restaurant. These differences are huge when competing with the rest of the Tex-Mex restaurants that don't offer these extras. These four items—the tortilla chips, red salsa, green salsa, and ice cream—add an additional 6 percent to our overall food cost, which is significant when you consider that our goal is to remain lower priced than our competitors. What helps us is to make sure we manage portions and waste.

Shortly after we opened up our second Gringo's location in La Porte, we were visited by several executives from another Mexican restaurant chain. One of the executives, whom I happened to know, asked me what the ice cream we gave away free to our guests was costing us in terms of the percentage of food costs.

Before I could even respond, he told me that they had tried it, and it added an additional X percent, and they didn't want to spend that much. Now, keep in mind that he was telling me all of this while he was enjoying one of our ice cream cones.

I just smiled.

Every business competes by comparison. So whenever one business offers more than another in their products or services, the consumer will notice the differences and decide where to spend their dollars.

THINK OUTSIDE THE TACO

While visiting one of the Gringo's locations, I once asked an assistant manager what he was working on. He answered, "I just got through finalizing the server schedule, and now I'm about to go into a pre-shift meeting."

During a visit to a different location, I asked the assistant manager on duty the same question and basically received the same answer.

While visiting yet another location a few days later, I did the same thing with that assistant manager. With a big grin on his face, he responded, "Sir, my team and I are serving up some of the most incredible Tex-Mex food ever made, and we're delivering it at a service level many of our guests have yet to experience!"

While the first two managers' responses were fine, the third response caught my attention. It is this kind of mindset that separates one manager from another, as well as one restaurant from another. This is what is necessary for a general manager to lead his fellow team members. The third manager was passionate about his duties and responsibilities. He didn't see his job as work; rather, he saw it as a mission to be the very best he could be. This kind of mindset is unique because not everyone sees their work this way.

Since then, we have conditioned our management team to align their mindset with this outlook of taking service to another level.

GOOD BUSINESS SENSE

Doing more than you're paid for can also apply to business strategy. Again, it comes back to planting money seeds. If you provide your customers with great value for your product or service, then the money will come.

Another company that I've learned from, particularly when it comes to providing great value to customers, is Walmart. How can a company advertise lower prices than the rest of its competitors and yet, at the same time, be one of the most successful companies in the world?

It didn't make sense to me. But selling a great product at lower prices was working for Walmart. I knew that if Gringo's was going to be a success in such a crowded field of Mexican restaurants, then we were going to have to sell a high-quality, great-tasting product and offer it at a lower price point than the majority of the competition.

To do that, we stay price-sensitive. We monitor our competitors' prices to ensure that our menu prices are at least equal to or lower than theirs. At the same time, we strive to serve food with superior ingredients.

Serving a high-quality product at a fair price has helped position Gringo's as one of the most successful Tex-Mex restaurant chains in the Houston market.

Many years ago, I toured a meat packing plant in Houston along with several of my executives. As we were walking through the facility, I noticed a huge seventy-gallon drum with a strange-looking material in it. It looked like dried dog food. It turns out it was an additive blended into ground beef as a filler. This filler also acts as a sponge and soaks up excess grease that otherwise would be discarded.

The product allows the restaurant to increase the yield of the ground beef used in their taco meat. For example, let's say they start off using one hundred pounds of 81/19 ground beef (81/19 indicates the meat-to-fat ratio) to prepare a batch of taco meat, what some restaurants call picadillo. After they brown the meat and before adding the spices, instead of draining approximately 10 percent of the grease or ten pounds and throwing it away, they would add ten pounds of filler to the same one hundred pounds of ground beef, therefore yielding 110 percent of prepared taco meat. The filler acts as a sponge and soaks up the excess grease that would otherwise be thrown away. So now, instead of throwing away the excess grease in the trash, the customer carries it out in their stomach when they leave the restaurant.

Speaking of fillers, "pink slime" was all over the news a few years ago. The substance I'm referring to is a finely textured beef additive made from cattle by-products collected after cattle are butchered into cuts such as steaks and roasts.

Using specialized equipment, the processors remove the fat from the trimmings and, in some cases, treat the meat for bacteria with ammonium hydroxide. It is then added to real ground beef (up to an astounding 15 percent) to provide more yield, thereby making it a more profitable product to sell. The USDA claims it is a safe, edible substance; however, they won't go as far as to approve it as a stand-alone product.

Unlike other restaurants that might not know where their meat truly comes from, Gringo's sources its ground beef directly from Iowa Beef Processors (IBP). We use a meat product that has a meat-to-fat ratio of 81 percent beef to 19 percent fat with *zero* fillers.

One of our suppliers tried to persuade us to purchase their label ground beef. Supposedly, it was IBP packing it. Our salesperson even went as far as to bring me a letter stating that IBP was indeed packing their product. However, I insisted they provide a letter *from* IBP stating that the two products were identical. As I suspected, I never received it.

The red flag for me was a simple question: How could the distributor offer their label ground beef (supposedly packed by the same processor we've done business with), state that it's the exact same product, and then be able to price it at 15 percent to 20 percent less than the processor's label?

The answer was easy. It was clearly not the same product, and Gringo's was *not* going to use it!

A restaurant must know the cost of every single ingredient it uses to prepare its food, especially high-cost items like beef, chicken, seafood, and so on. Once it knows these numbers (which can fluctuate weekly), it can then build a menu around this information. Many restaurateurs, though, focus mainly on their bottom line and, as a result, may look for ways to cut corners. The easiest way to cut costs is to purchase lower-quality, less expensive ingredients.

For instance, most restaurants will use the cheapest oil they can source simply because they do not view cooking oil as a "real" ingredient. But there's a very good reason why we use a high-quality, more expensive cooking oil at Gringo's. Cooking oil affects just about every single item we serve, from our enchiladas and taco shells to our french fries and tortilla chips. I've had many guests over the years tell me that they really enjoy our food and it's better than most restaurants, but they don't know why. They can't pinpoint exactly what it is. I truly believe that if a high-quality oil is used, cooking oil alone can make a simple meal much more enjoyable. Using the highest-quality ingredients is not an area we compromise on.

At Gringo's, we focus not only on the quality of ingredients that go into a dish but on the appearance as well. For example, one of our most popular entrees is the Veracruz plate, which consists of fajitas and shrimp brochette. For our shrimp brochette, we take a large, clean, and deveined piece of shrimp, a slice of jalapeño, and a strip of cheese, wrap it with a strip of bacon, and grill it on the flat top griddle.

When we first started making it, we noticed that before the shrimp were fully cooked, the Monterey Jack cheese we were using inside the bacon would melt away, and you couldn't really tell there was any cheese in it to begin with. Not only was the cheese important to the taste of the item, but it also had to be visually appealing. So we searched for another cheese that would keep its integrity throughout the grilling process and still be able to be seen after the shrimp and bacon were both fully cooked.

The cheese we found was a Mexican cheese called *panela*, and it has been a game changer. Although the panela cheese is considerably higher in cost, it doesn't matter. What matters is we saw the opportunity to improve our food no matter the cost. What was more important was achieving a product all of us can be proud to serve.

Ultimately, we discovered that since this panela cheese didn't melt away while being cooked on the griddle, we didn't have to use the same size piece as before. Therefore our cost for this dish didn't increase. We were able to deliver a much better product, and we didn't have to increase our prices.

It is the yield, not the price that a restaurant pays for ingredients, that ultimately determines its food cost. Here's another example of how that works: Every ingredient a restaurant purchases is priced by the pound or by the count. For example, take two cases of individual sugar packets (two thousand count)—one brand is priced at $9 per case, while another is $11. Your first inclination would be to purchase the $9 case and save a couple of bucks. But if you weigh each one and find out that the cheaper one weighs six pounds and the costlier one weighs eight pounds, and you do the math, you will see that the $11 case is a better deal.

This is what the habit of doing more than what you're paid for does: It changes your focus from how much money you can make to what you sell. And as you can see, using higher-cost ingredients hasn't hurt our bottom line—it has helped increase it. This habit forces the competition to do the same to keep up.

There will always be an inferior, less expensive way of doing things, but quality matters, and there is almost never a shortcut to achieving it. Doing more than you're paid for as a business allows you to separate your brand from the rest of the competition because quality has a way of standing out. As we celebrate our thirty-first year in business, I'm proud to say that every food item that we've ever changed has always been for a higher grade in quality. While a lot of restaurants focus on the bottom line, we focus on the top of the plate.

To-Go Items

1. Plant service and harvest money.

2. Every "something extra" you do for others is a money seed.

3. Doing more than what you're paid for changes your focus from how much money you make to what you sell—and forces your competition to do the same.

CHAPTER 2

Always Look for Ways to Improve

~~~~~~

Perfection is not attainable, but if we chase perfection, we can catch excellence.

—ATTRIBUTED TO VINCE LOMBARDI

S uccess is a terrible teacher in and of itself because it will give a person the illusion that they can do no wrong. Over the years, I have seen too many business owners believe that their success is the reason never to change because how else would you explain their success? Well, for starters, success is not a destination that you arrive at—it is a mindset that says there is always room for improvement. Consumers' demands are constantly changing and evolving; therefore, businesses must do the same to remain competitive and relevant. A business's longevity will depend entirely on its ability to progress continuously, looking for ways to improve the customer's experience.

In the restaurant business, in particular, we are always evaluating our products and processes for ways to improve them. In 2010, for example, we were developing a new Tex-Mex restaurant concept named Jimmy Changas (a play on the Mexican dish chimichangas). I wanted to make sure we gave Jimmy Changas its own identity, separate from our familiar Gringo's down the street.

Obviously, the menu was one way to do that, so we introduced subtle yet distinct differences between Jimmy Changas and Gringo's. At Jimmy Changas, we serve white queso versus yellow queso at Gringo's. The Mexican rice at Jimmy Changas is a traditional Spanish rice, and at Gringo's, it is yellow (chicken stock base). There are a few other items that separate the two brands, the biggest one being Jimmy Changas has an outdoor playground, which makes it very family-friendly. The kids get to play while the parents enjoy a delicious margarita on the patio.

Over the years, I had kept a running list of menu items that I wished we could serve at Gringo's but knew we couldn't because those items would slow down the kitchen. Jimmy Changas presented a great opportunity to create a new menu that included these items.

As we were developing these recipes, one of the items that made me put on the brakes was our Tex-Mex enchilada gravy. Our enchilada gravy is a roux-like sauce that includes Gebhardt brand chili powder (the gold standard of chili powders), as well as other spices and ingredients. Although we prepared it similarly to most other Mexican restaurants, including Gringo's, I realized upon further scrutiny that there was room for improvement. Rather than use beef trimmings from the outside skirt used for our fajitas, we decided to use lean ground beef, making it a leaner and cleaner product by removing a substantial amount of saturated fat. We also rolled out this change immediately at all our Gringo's locations. We even modified the recipe to reduce a substantial amount of sodium. This decision forced me to have a major paradigm shift in my philosophy when it came to every single ingredient we use throughout our restaurants: If I won't eat it, I won't serve it.

Taste testing every new dish we serve requires input from our executive team, our culinary operations team, and our marketing department. This allows us to be engaged with every stage of what's required to roll out a new menu item across all twenty-one Gringo's and Jimmy Changas locations. The only time we ever look at or consider changing any ingredient is if it will improve the quality of the item we're considering changing and if it will still allow us to maintain an affordable price point.

It is important in business, no matter how successful you become, to always question everything your company does. Most restaurateurs focus mainly on their bottom-line profit. While, obviously, the bottom line is important to remaining in business, I believe what is most important is to focus more on what is served on the plates. If a business owner focuses more on the top of the plate instead of their profit, their bottom line will improve automatically.

CONTINUOUS IMPROVEMENT

I've always told myself that no matter how many restaurants we open, I never want to feel disconnected from our customers. After all, they are the main driver of every decision we make in our business, and we cannot make good decisions if we are disconnected from them. I always go back to the feeling of gratitude I experienced when that very first car pulled into our parking lot on the first day of business at Gringo's. It is a feeling I will continue to remind myself of because of its impact on me and our company's success.

One way we stay connected to our customers is by responding to their needs. We do that through the process of continuous improvement. The Japanese philosophy of continuous improvement is embodied in the word *kaizen*: *kai* means "change," and *zen* means "good"—good change. If you're the kind of person who, no matter how well you perform a job, always asks how you could have done it better, then you're on the right track.

When it comes to making continuous improvements for the sake of our customers, one person who has long inspired me is Mark Cuban, owner of the NBA Dallas Mavericks and one of the investor "sharks" on ABC's TV show *Shark Tank*. In 2013, I had the privilege of meeting Mark in Los Angeles on the set of *Shark Tank*. Mark was on my bucket list of people that I'd always wanted to meet; I see a lot of myself in him. The major difference, of course, is that he is a billionaire, and I am not! He is also, in my opinion, the nicest shark around.

One of his quotes that stands out to me is, "Treat your customers like they own you. Because they do."[3] In Mark Cuban's book, *How to Win at the Sport of Business*, he lays out what I consider to be one very important quality every successful businessperson must have: the ability to remain connected to your customers.

Case in point, Mark chooses to sit in the $2–$10 nosebleed seats at Dallas Mavericks games; he wants to see the game through the eyes of the fans. Also, when he visits his Landmark Theaters, he doesn't call ahead to receive special treatment. Instead, he will stand in line to purchase his drink and popcorn to experience what his customers experience.

I have on many occasions told our staff that the most important person in their lives is the one who pays their bills, and that's a very factual statement. After all, no customer, no revenue. Every single guest who walks through our front doors at Gringo's and Jimmy Changas and patronizes our restaurant is vitally important to our success.

The last word in Sam Walton's autobiography, *Made in America*, is "customer." I am sure Mr. Walton intentionally did this in hopes of the reader understanding who the most

---

3   John Brandon, "20 Best Mark Cuban Quotes on Finding Success," *Inc.*, July 21, 2015, https://www.inc.com/john-brandon/20-best-mark-cuban-quotes-on-finding-success.html/.

important person in business is. Without the *customer*, no business would exist.

What I have observed over my many years of working in the restaurant industry is that, all too often, the independent operator begins to leave the customer out of the loop. In other words, the owner begins to believe that they, not the customer, are the reason for their business's success.

I do not want to take anything away from the hard work and creativity of a successful restaurant operator. However, the day you take more credit for your success than you should is the day you enter the slippery road to failure.

I have known several restaurant owners who have reached unprecedented heights of success in their business, only to wind up going broke and losing everything they own.

Why?

Simply put, they forgot what got them there in the first place—the customer.

But continuous improvement is more than just keeping the customer happy. Our staff is vitally important too. If we take care of our team members, our team members will take care of our guests. Beyond paying our team members a competitive wage and instilling a culture of continuous improvement, we also provide a supportive work environment. As part of that environment, we provide incentives to our staff in various ways to enhance their lives outside work. For instance, we offer scholarships to hourly team members, suite ticket giveaways to area sporting events and concerts, and international trips for managers, general managers, and executives. Plus, we have given an annual Christmas gift or bonus to every single team member for the past twenty-five years.

We have a full-time pastor, Sam Hernandez, who travels to each location to minister to team members who may be facing all sorts of personal issues. We established the Tex-Mex Legacy Foundation in 2019 to help our team members who may be dealing with a personal crisis, such as needing financial assistance to repair their automobile or help to relocate to a new apartment building and furnish it with brand-new furniture after a fire destroyed the one they were living in. It is important that an employer be there for their employees in times of need.

BUILDING GUEST RELATIONSHIPS

We serve thousands of meals each day at Gringo's. And no matter how many meals we get right, the ones that we don't are the most important. When Outback Steakhouse opened in the late 1980s, its slogan was "No rules, just right."[4] I'm sure their slogan was based on something similar to our first core value: building guest relationships one meal at a time. Every guest, every meal we serve is vitally important to our success and longevity.

The restaurant industry deals with two of the most volatile things in the world, people and food, and both need constant attention. If Gringo's plans on celebrating another thirty years

---

4   Outback Steakhouse, "All about Outback Steakhouse," accessed November 9, 2023, https://www.outback.com/about-us/.

in business, then we have to always look for ways to improve our guests' experience by questioning every single thing we do. Most independent restaurateurs are egotistical by nature, one reason being that they take so much pride in what they serve that they believe it to be a better product than it actually is.

Pride has a way of clouding a restaurateur's point of view. Anytime a guest has an issue with their food, we must do everything in our power to make them happy before they leave our restaurant. A guest complaint is merely an opportunity to show them that they matter. Eating out isn't cheap, and there's nothing worse than feeling cheated by paying for a meal you didn't enjoy. Anytime I receive an email from a guest with a complaint, I stop what I'm doing and respond by first apologizing and then saying that we'll make it right by returning their money—and we'll usually follow up with sending them a gift card to enjoy on their next visit.

If you want to succeed in business, you will need to learn the art of resolving guest complaints. We once received a complaint from a frequent guest who was disappointed to discover that we added shredded carrots and purple cabbage to our lettuce mix (used in our tacos and chalupas for visual accent). Although we'd been doing this for several years, this was the first complaint we'd ever received about it. The guest commented, "Whatever happened to just lettuce, tomato, and cheese?"

When I first read the comment, my automatic response was defensive. But I stopped for a second and reminded myself this guest was my boss. If they are unhappy with how we prepare something, they are entitled to their opinion. The ultimate lesson for me was this: If we are able to accommodate our guests in a way that does not interrupt the quality of service to our other guests, then we should do whatever it takes to accommodate them—especially if it keeps them coming back. For this particular guest, we gladly switched the lettuce mix to make them happy.

A few years ago, the *Houston Chronicle*, in its "Whine & Dine" section, included an example of how *not* to handle a guest situation. A person who liked to frequent different area restaurants wrote in about their experience at one place—and an issue they had with the bill. More than the issue with the bill itself was how management handled the problem.

The customer had ordered a bottle of wine from the printed menu that included the price. But when the bill came, the person was charged $20 more than what was advertised. After the person asked for it to be corrected, the waiter returned to say that the price on the menu was incorrect, but they could adjust the price, which was still $7 more than the printed price. The customer refused to pay the difference and finally received a corrected bill. In their letter, the customer firmly stated that they would not return to that restaurant.

My reaction to reading this was, "Wow!" If there is one thing a businessperson must be able to do, it is this: See the bigger picture! In this particular case, what's more important—$7 or a satisfied customer who may spend hundreds if not thousands of dollars at your establishment for years to come?

Tilman Fertitta, owner of Houston-based restaurant giant Landry's Inc., was once quoted as saying, "There are no spare customers."[5] And he is not kidding. I don't care how many restaurants we continue to open. I will always think back to January 11, 1993, and the gratitude I felt when I saw that first car pull into the parking lot to give us a try. They say that failure is where we learn our most important lessons. Failure is what also allows us to understand how meaningful success can be. I learned that fact many years ago and am a better businessman because of it.

JUDGE NOT, LEST YOU BE JUDGED

One of the ways that I get inspired to improve in every area is by going out to eat and seeing what other restaurants are doing. I look for new trends, service level, atmosphere, food presentation, or anything that is being done well.

However, when my wife, Monica, and I are out having dinner with friends who are not in the restaurant business, and something goes wrong with our food, service, or both, our friends expect me to have some sort of Gordon Ramsey moment and go off on the establishment, giving my so-called expert opinion of the situation. To their surprise, I never do.

The reason is quite simple. Anything that can go wrong during one of my dining out experiences can easily happen at one of our restaurants. If there is one business I want to stay completely out of, it is the business of criticizing other restaurants.

Most successful restaurateurs I know feel the same way I do

5   Tilman Fertitta, *Shut Up and Listen! Hard Business Truths That Will Help You Succeed* (New York: Harper Collins Leadership, 2019), 20.

about critiquing fellow competitors. It is one of those unspoken and understood laws of respect. I guess you'd have to have been in the restaurant business to understand this point truly.

The Texas Restaurant Association's slogan is "Eating out is fun!"[6] Keeping food fun is one of our top priorities at Gringo's. Because there are so many different ways food can be prepared, experiencing all the different varieties is like going on a delicious adventure. If I were to eat at an Italian restaurant, the last thing I would want is food that tastes exactly like a competing Italian restaurant down the street. In my opinion, that would be very boring, and I'm sure many of you would agree.

PHILOSOPHY OF EXCELLENCE

One of the most important lessons that I ever learned from working for my father was seeing him regularly remodeling his restaurants. This particular lesson showed me the value of constantly reinvesting in my properties.

You don't want your business, particularly a public-facing one like a restaurant, to ever become stale by looking dated or worn out. If a business wants to experience any longevity, then it must not only maintain consistency in its products or services but also keep the facility well maintained at all times.

Maintenance is a prime target for business owners looking to save money. There's an unintended ripple effect that happens

6   Texas Restaurant Association, "About TRA," accessed October 25, 2023, https://www.txrestaurant.org/about/.

whenever a business owner kicks the can down the road, so to speak, and does not keep the facilities as well maintained as they should be. Usually, the first people to notice are the employees, followed almost immediately by the customers. Most employees, when they notice that an operator is not keeping the facilities up to par, will think to themselves that if the owner doesn't care about how the facility looks, then why should they?

Most operators cut maintenance first because it is the easiest and quickest way to reduce costs and drive those dollars straight to the bottom line. A friend of mine who worked for a homebuilder would always tell new homeowners that on the very first day they moved in, their new home would be in a constant state of deterioration.

The Original Gringo's building that we opened in 1993 had already been added onto six times before we decided to start fresh by constructing a new building on the same property in 2004. During those first eleven years in business, we would always look for ways to improve our facility. At every opportunity (meaning every time we had the cash on hand), we would try to improve the restaurant in one fashion or another. We relocated the walk-in cooler outside to give us more space in the kitchen; we added onto the building to increase our storeroom capacity; we added an additional dining room; we expanded our foyer to accommodate more guests waiting for a table during peak hours; we built a small corporate office; we even added new restrooms. And we did all of these things despite ultimately tearing down the building in 2004 to build the one that is there today.

In 2022, we were at it again. I made the executive decision to remodel a large section of the Original Gringo's restaurant. At first, we were only going to enlarge our to-go room but discovered that during the 2020 pandemic, curbside service was more appealing to our guests than having them get out of their vehicles and walk inside. So we scrapped that idea.

I felt that since the Original Gringo's is where it all began, then it should look like we are as proud of it as we are of our newer models. We completely remodeled two-thirds of the restaurant, which included one large dining room, a private dining room, and the bar area. The first and second phases of the remodel were completed just in time to celebrate our thirtieth anniversary on January 11, 2023.

On a smaller scale, there are always plenty of continuous improvements (many never seen by our customers) to make at our various facilities. But we do it anyway. In a great book I read a few years back titled *Inside the Magic Kingdom*, author Tom Connellan writes, "How often should Disney repaint the hitching posts at Disney World? Most of us would answer this question by thinking about the lifespan of a coat of paint, exploring the costs of extra coats, and studying the price and reliability of various paint manufacturers. Or, in the case of Disney, you can paint the posts every night after the park closes."[7]

Paying this much attention to one single detail says more about

---

7   Tom Connellan, *Inside the Magic Kingdom: Seven Keys to Disney's Success* (Peak Performance Press, 1997), 29.

a company's philosophy of excellence than anything else. Will a visitor to Disney World ever notice that the posts are in perfect condition? Probably not. What makes this standard of excellence more meaningful than the paint itself is that it sends a message to every employee that if a company is willing to pay this much attention to something like a post, what about everything else they do?

Another example of striving for excellence comes from a hero of mine—Dave Thomas, the founder of Wendy's Hamburgers. When Dave volunteered for the U.S. Army at age eighteen, he was a mess sergeant responsible for two thousand meals per day. One of the many lessons he learned in the army was the importance of keeping everything spotless. He witnessed how important it was just to keep all the buildings on the base freshly painted at all times.[8]

A few years after the Clauss family franchised several Kentucky Fried Chicken restaurants, Dave was given part ownership of four underperforming units. He was assigned the task of helping turn them around. He did just that by applying a lot of what he learned during his time in the army.[9]

Dave also worked closely with Colonel Harland Sanders to help make KFC more profitable by reducing the number of items on the menu and instead focusing on a signature dish. Dave also convinced Col. Sanders to appear in his commercials. Dave did

---

8   Dave Thomas with Ron Beyma and Mary Maroon Gelpi, *Dave's Way: A New Approach to Old-Fashioned Success* (Dublin, OH: Dave Thomas Foundation for Adoption, 2016).

9   Thomas, Beyma, and Gelpi, *Dave's Way.*

not believe a business should pay someone else to talk about their product if the only reason they're doing so is because they're being paid for it. That is why, besides the "Where's the beef?" lady, Dave appeared in all the Wendy's commercials.[10]

Soon after Dave helped turn around the four struggling KFC restaurants, the entire company was purchased, and Dave's share was $1.5 million. With that money, Dave opened the very first Wendy's in Columbus, Ohio, in 1969 and grew it to become the third-largest hamburger chain in the world.[11]

When asked why Wendy's hamburger patties are square, Dave would always give the same answer: "Because we don't cut corners!"[12] In reality, using a square patty versus a round patty allowed them to maximize the griddle space on the flat top.

Like Dave Thomas, we don't cut corners—not when it comes to our food or keeping our restaurants in top condition. As mentioned earlier, we're constantly making continuous improvements. For example, the flooring in a lot of our restaurant kitchens consists of square red quarry tiles. Although we choose to use an expensive epoxy grout, it inevitably wears away over time because of its constant contact with soap and grease.

There are only two options a restaurant has whenever the epoxy grout is eaten away. It can either ignore the problem, or it can regrout the tiles. Most restaurants ignore the problem. I

---

10 Thomas, Beyma, and Gelpi, *Dave's Way.*

11 Kyle Schurman, "The Untold Truth of Dave Thomas," *Mashed*, March 9, 2023, https://www .mashed.com/132710/the-untold-truth-of-dave-thomas/; Thomas, Beyma, and Gelpi, *Dave's Way.*

12 Thomas, Beyma, and Gelpi, *Dave's Way*, 9.

know because I've seen it time and time again whenever I visit other restaurants.

At Gringo's and Jimmy Changas, we have to regrout our kitchen floors every couple of years or so. If we don't do it, water will inevitably get underneath the tiles through the worn-out grout, causing the tiles to come loose, exposing large sections of the concrete floor, and creating a whole new set of problems. If our maintenance department doesn't immediately address and repair the problem, it will only get worse, costing more than if we simply regrouted it.

I want our kitchen floors always to be well maintained no matter what it costs, mainly because the cost to repair it never really goes away; it is just delayed. Our company spends a lot of money yearly regrouting our kitchen floors, and that's perfectly fine with me. To me, it's also about taking pride in everything we do because I know our employees notice and appreciate these things, especially if they've ever worked at another restaurant.

Businesses compete in many different ways. This is just one example of how important it is to have a philosophy of excellence and to always, always look for ways to improve.

To-Go Items

1. A business's longevity depends on its ability to evolve continuously.

2. No matter how successful you become, always question everything your company does.

3. If a business doesn't first focus on the needs of its employees, there won't be any customers.

4. If you want to succeed in business, learn the art of resolving complaints.

5. When employees notice their employer not keeping facilities well maintained, they will think, "If the owner doesn't care, why should I?"

CHAPTER 3

Guard Your Reputation

~~~~~~

It takes twenty years to build a reputation and five minutes to ruin it. If you think about that, you'll do things differently.

—WARREN BUFFETT, *Warren Buffett on Business*

The first time I ever heard the phrase "bad reputation" was in junior high school. The words were often used to describe boys and girls who were suspected of either doing drugs or having sex. In 1980, American recording artist Joan Jett and the Blackhearts released a song called "Bad Reputation." The main chorus of the song declares that they just don't care about their reputations.

I guess that's fine if you really don't care where you're heading in life. But one thing is for sure: If you go into business and want to be successful, your reputation *does* matter. It is extremely important, perhaps the most valuable thing you will ever own because you are the only one who is in control of it.

One way to protect your reputation is never to have it questioned. One way of doing that is to always be transparent, honest, and open in your communications. Another is keeping your word. When you say you'll do something, follow through on it. Being told, "Your word is good enough," is a point of pride for me.

I think back to all those times when it mattered whether I made the bank payment on time or was paying our vendors within terms. In other words, have I kept my word? As individuals, we must always, no matter the cost, keep our word. Because you know what? It does matter. The short-term gain will never outweigh the long-term cost. Your reputation in life will always follow you wherever you go, and because of social media, it will follow you no matter where you end up.

Being in business is nothing more than a test to see if a person is capable of handling the responsibilities that come with the territory. I take much pride in the fact that our company is current with all its banknotes, payroll taxes, property taxes, vendors, and the like. Remember, don't put too much emphasis on the material aspects of your life. Your greatest asset has always been and will always be your reputation.

A TIMELY REPUTATION

The phrase "a day late and a dollar short" is assumed to come from the days of the Great Depression. I hate to be late to anything for any reason. As a matter of fact, I am most often early to many events I attend. Fortunately, my position allows me to have a flexible schedule. My wife, Monica, often makes fun of me for wanting to show up early to events, especially at social gatherings. She tells me that it is okay to be "fashionably late." I don't know about that—I just know I like to be early.

There are only two individuals who have been with Gringo's since its first day of operation—head cook Hugo Olvera and me. I can honestly say Gringo's would not be the company it is today were it not for Hugo joining me at Gringo's. One of Hugo's characteristics is his ability to be very punctual.

Hugo's company vehicle has an EZ Tag (a tollway tag) on it. Every morning, on his way to work, Hugo crosses the ship channel via the toll bridge, and I am always amazed by his consistent timing for traveling through the tollbooth. The EZ Tag statement always reads crossing times of 6:31 a.m., 6:33 a.m., and 6:30 a.m. He is *always* within a five-minute window of time. And did I mention that in the thirty years Hugo has worked for Gringo's, he has never missed a day of work?

They just don't make them like Hugo anymore.

To me, punctuality is extremely important in the restaurant business. For us to meet and exceed our guests' expectations, everything my team members do revolves around time. As the team leader, I set the example by being punctual with everything so that my team members will follow suit.

LEAVE NO ROOM FOR DOUBTS

If you are going to grow your business, you will more than likely have to borrow money along the way. When I purchased the land in La Porte from a local businessman named Bruce Angel to build the second Gringo's location, I decided to go ahead and purchase the remaining two acres of the land that he owned next to it. He was gracious enough to owner-finance the property for me. Since I knew Bruce was old school, I made sure never to be late with a payment. Instead of mailing the check each month and risking it being even a day late, I drove it over to his office two or three days before it was due so I could hand deliver it to him in person. I never wanted to give Bruce any doubt that he made the right decision in financing the property for me.

When I worked for my father at El Toro in the '80s, he often faced a lot of rejection whenever he tried to secure a commercial loan. In one instance, he hired an accountant to help him secure a $150,000 loan from a Houston area bank. Every bank requires certain items from the borrower to process and approve a loan. You never want to provide any documentation that will cost you up-front money until you know for certain that the loan you're applying for will be approved.

For example, my father did not want to order an MAI appraisal without knowing for sure he was approved. An MAI appraisal is the gold standard of valuations for real estate. If an MAI appraiser states that a property has a valuation of X dollars, you can literally take that to the bank. But these appraisals are not cheap.

My dad met with our accountant, who assured him that the loan was approved and there would be no issue. The bank just needed him to order an MAI appraisal of the property he was using as collateral to approve the loan formally.

We were going to be charged $5,000 from the appraiser. Before the appraisal was completed, though, we noticed a change in the demeanor of the banker who had promised my dad that, once the appraisal was complete, they would be able to close on the loan, and he would receive the loan proceeds.

Sure enough, once the appraisal was completed, this banker was no longer with the bank, and my dad's loan request ended up being denied. My father was obviously upset, and he gave me the awkward task of giving the accountant the bad news that he was going to have to share in half of the cost of the appraisal. At the time, I felt bad having to tell the accountant that he was responsible for half the invoice. But at the same time, a person should not make promises that are out of their control and could potentially end up costing another person money.

MAKING THINGS RIGHT

When you do mess up—and you will—what's important is how you respond. That can make all the difference when it comes to your reputation.

In business, you will face situations where a simple misunderstanding can end up causing a relationship to go south. Case in point: Shortly after we opened the Gringo's in La Porte, we needed to have a couple of custom stainless steel items fabricated. It was a tube to hold a sleeve of seventy-five plastic cups that would allow a cook to pull out one at a time. I reached out to a longtime friend of the family, Bart Salinas, who owned a successful fabrication shop called Bemis Sheet Metal in Baytown, Texas. Although most of his work included large jobs for Exxon, he would always help us out if we ever needed a small, custom piece fabricated.

After I showed Bart what I needed fabricated, I called him up to ask how much it would cost for two of them. He told me he could do it "for a hundred dollars each." Since it sounded very reasonable, I told Bart, "Go ahead and make me four of them."

A few days later, Bart called to tell me that the four stainless steel sleeves were ready to be picked up. I asked him how much I owed since I figured there would be sales tax included. He said the grand total was "one thousand, six hundred, and ninety-six dollars."

I said, "*What?!* You said you could do them for a hundred dollars each."

He replied, "I said I could do them for *four hundred dollars each*, and I'm not letting them leave my shop for anything less than that."

Well, I learned a few lessons that day. For one, "for a hundred dollars each" and "four hundred dollars each" sound very similar over the phone. I also learned to always get a written proposal before having any work performed for our business.

Since I accepted full responsibility for misunderstanding what I heard over the phone, I paid him the full amount. Today, those same sleeves are available at the restaurant supply house for sixty dollars each, not four *hundred* each! Lesson learned. Move on. Salvage a relationship; it's more valuable than money.

A few years ago, my wife and I built our very first custom house in Houston. We had already been living in the same neighborhood since 2006. We soon discovered this great corner lot for sale, so we decided to purchase it and build our dream house. We hired a dream team to design it, build it, and decorate it. We hired the contractor based on a referral from another well-known architect. He basically said that if he ever built a house, he would only hire this contractor because of his work ethic and reputation.

Once the construction began, my wife and I met the interior designer at a nearby stone yard to pick out the stone flooring that would be installed throughout the first floor. We decided on one called Dublin Gray, Historic Finish that came out of a quarry in India. This was in May 2019. The flooring contractor started the installation in January 2020, and it took approximately four months to complete. As each section was installed, the subcontractor covered it with brown construction paper to protect it from being stained or damaged by all the different trades working in the house.

When the installation was complete, they removed the paper to reveal the flooring. Monica and I were in shock. Not only did the flooring not look like what we had picked out, but there was also no uniform look to the rooms where it was installed. In the family room, the stone finish was very rough. In the formal dining room, the floor finish had several different shades of color. And in the formal living room, there were all these small, round, one-inch spots that looked like someone had dropped paint on the floor. (These spots turned out to be trapped volcanic gasses from millions of years ago.) The new stone flooring throughout the house looked terrible.

When we picked out the flooring, we were told there would be slight variations in the stone, so we were stuck between a rock and a hard place. Literally. We met with the entire construction and design team to see what our options were, and none of them were good. After the meeting, I was walking to my car with the construction supervisor when he either willingly or accidentally told me, "Russell, you do know that the stone we installed did not come from the stone yard where y'all picked it out, right?"

No, we did *not* know that. In the end, the contractor acknowledged that he made a mistake. Apparently, there were discussions between the contractor, subcontractor, and others about getting the stone from another stone yard because, according to the contractor, they could get it sooner. The problem, of course, was that they never informed us; nor did we ever give them approval to get the stone elsewhere.

The issue was eventually resolved to our satisfaction; it just delayed the project by almost five months. The contractor, along with the subcontractor, ended up replacing the floor throughout the entire house at their expense. The job was made extra difficult because the walls were already plastered to the stone floor, and tearing out the floor could easily damage the plaster on the walls.

I share this story because of how easily a business's good reputation can be affected. I hired this contractor because of another person's recommendation. I did not know anything about him prior to hiring him to build our custom home. But, in the end, he lived up to the reputation of honoring his word and making things right. A business's reputation will *always* be more valuable than *any* dollar amount that may be in dispute.

Let me repeat that. A business's reputation will *always* be more valuable than *any* dollar amount that may be in dispute.

Everyone's goal in life should be to master the art of dispute resolution. Taking a step backward isn't the end of the world when you are confident that you will eventually be taking two or more steps forward. Resolving disputes is an art form many people in business truly don't seem to understand today. Many people approach business with a win-lose mentality rather than a win-win attitude. The art is to get through a dispute without tarnishing your name, whether the dispute was justified or not. Sometimes, it is okay to lose at first because you will win eventually if you're able to see the bigger picture of where you're headed in your business or career.

TRANSPARENCY AND HONESTY ARE KEY

If your dream is to one day open a new business and your goal is to be around for a while, start by developing strong relationships with other people that are built on candor, honesty, mutual respect, and—most importantly—integrity. It is a process that takes time and requires patience. The result will be a future built on such a strong foundation that these relationships will become an integral part of your success. A prime example of this is a man by the name of Hugh Ruggles. A commercial real estate broker, Hugh would become an integral part of our success thanks to his transparency and integrity.

A couple of years after opening our second Gringo's location in La Porte, Joel Perkins (the general manager at that location) told me that Jerry Perkins, his uncle and a commercial real estate broker, had been wanting to show us a six-acre tract of land in Texas City near the Gulf Greyhound Park to consider building a third Gringo's location.

Joel kept reminding me about the land for sale until we finally set up a meeting with his uncle. We drove out to the site on a February afternoon in 1999, and we met his uncle at a Waffle House next door to the for-sale property. After our meeting, Joel and I decided to drive around the area to get a feel for what it looked like.

As we drove around, we noticed a building for sale in front of the mall nearby. It turned out to be a closed-down Red Lobster that had been all boarded up for a couple of years. We called the number listed on the "For Sale" sign, and it so happened that the person listed on the sign was already on his way to the property. His name was Hugh Ruggles. Hugh was on his way there to show the property to another restaurant operator from Galveston. Coincidentally, they had already submitted a letter of intent to purchase the building for $750,000, and it was accepted by Red Lobster. Fortunately for us, the potential buyer never showed up for the meeting. I told Hugh I would match his offer and close on the property in sixty days. He told me to submit a letter of intent, and he'd make it happen.

What I really liked about this particular property was that it already had the basic infrastructure of a full-service restaurant in place. Once we closed on the Red Lobster building, we spent another half-million dollars renovating it. We opened our third Gringo's location on August 2, 1999, less than five months after Joel and I first walked through it. That's a quick turnaround by any standard.

However, there is a better part to this story. Since it was Joel's uncle who was really the one responsible for getting us out in the area to look at real estate, Joel decided to ask Hugh to see if he'd consider sharing his sales commission with Uncle Jerry.

Hugh didn't hesitate for one second and said, "Absolutely!"

In my opinion, that spoke volumes about Hugh because we had only known each other for a couple of months. Seeing the bigger picture is very difficult for some people, especially when the picture involves giving up some of their money. Obviously, Hugh had no idea if he would ever represent us again, so that made what Hugh did for Joel's uncle extra special because he had no ulterior motives when he said, "Absolutely!"

Because of what Hugh did for Joel's uncle and because there was never any hesitation whatsoever on his part to share his commission, Hugh has gone on to represent us in at least eight more land deals over the past couple of decades, earning him well over a million dollars in commissions.

Another example of Hugh's integrity on our behalf happened in 2002. That year, an On the Border restaurant building in Stafford, Texas, was for sale. The asking price was $1.6 million. The building was in terrible condition because it had been vacant for over seven years. Two reasons the property hadn't sold were that On the Border was still making the monthly lease payments and that the freeway directly in front of the building had been under construction for several years.

I wanted to purchase this building to open up our fifth Gringo's. Once again, this property had all the infrastructure we needed. I reached out to Hugh to see about buying it. But he told me that despite the building's terrible condition, the landlord (whose offices were in Chicago) would not entertain any offer for less than what it was listed for. Plus, Hugh let me know that there was already another Mexican restaurant interested in buying it at full price.

Good thing for me, Hugh didn't like the other buyer. Apparently, this potential buyer wanted Hugh to do something unethical to make the deal happen. Hugh later told me that he has had a great relationship with Brinker (the parent company of On the Border) and that he would never do anything to compromise that relationship. So Hugh went out of his way to make sure that the deal ended up in our favor.

Once we closed on the property and were now the landlord, On the Border paid us $200,000 to get out of the lease, so our net purchase price was $1.4 million. We spent another $1.6 million to remodel it. When it comes to growing a business, there are no shortcuts. Trying to expand your business using unethical methods is never a good idea.

In 2002, shortly after we had acquired the property in Stafford to open up our fifth location, I received an early phone call one Saturday morning from a subcontractor installing floor tile. He told me he smelled smoke but was unable to find the source. We did not want to take any chances, so we immediately called the fire department.

When the firefighters arrived, they also could not locate the source of the smoke, so they started tearing into a few of the walls using their axes. After about thirty minutes, they finally found it. Apparently, the fireplace igniter above the drop ceiling had malfunctioned and started to burn a huge structural wood beam. Because the flame wasn't receiving enough oxygen, it was simply smoldering the beam. We caught it in time and felt like we had dodged a bullet.

I quickly called my insurance agent and told him what had just happened. He drove over immediately to the restaurant to assess the damage and help us file a small claim. He appeared more frazzled about what had just happened than we were, and we soon discovered why.

This agent had already insured our other four locations; Stafford was his fifth. During the process of making this claim, we discovered that our agent was self-insuring all our policies. He was collecting and keeping 100 percent of insurance premiums paid by his clients. If one of them needed to make a small claim, no problem—he'd just pay it out of his own pocket. The problem was if there were a catastrophic claim by one of his clients, he would not have the money to pay it out to continue the illegal scheme.

This small incident at Stafford exposed our agent's fraudulent practices. He ended up being charged with fraud and sent to prison. His name and reputation are ruined forever. It's almost impossible to come back from something like that. No one will ever trust him again.

Apparently, his vice was going to strip clubs and buying the dancers' attention with his clients' insurance premiums. Just imagine how successful this person would be today if he had simply operated his business ethically. We have twenty-two restaurants that this agent would have in his portfolio if only he had been ethical.

Our fourth core value—developing a relationship of trust with our vendors—is about believing that our vendors are good and honest and will never take advantage of us under any circumstances. We, in return, will pay them promptly so they can continue looking out for our company's best interest. It is a bond unlike any other because when there is trust between two businesses that share the same philosophy of fairness and respect, knowing that each party wants to grow and succeed together, the sky's the limit.

GREATER AS A WHOLE

I've been involved with the Texas Restaurant Association (TRA) for many years. The saying "The whole is greater than the sum of its parts" definitely applies to this organization when it comes to the power all of us in the restaurant business can have when we're trying to influence legislation that can benefit restaurateurs across the Lone Star State. If it were not for the TRA working on behalf of its members and the restaurant industry, many of us would be paying higher sales and liquor taxes.

During the pandemic of 2020, restaurants across the entire state of Texas and the nation were forced to close their dining rooms and offer only to-go meals, curbside. Our sales dropped 75 percent overnight. Our company had to regroup and plan for how to survive this new reality. Straightaway, we went to a very limited menu and set up an execution plan to serve 100 percent of our business using only takeout.

Since every restaurant was in the same dilemma, our senior VP of operations at the time, Danny Hanks, went to work immediately to procure as much to-go packaging as possible. Our fourth core value—developing a relationship of trust with our vendors—helped put us in a priority position to secure enough packaging to continue serving our guests. I'm sure our reputation of paying our vendors promptly helped us during this difficult time.

The TRA was instrumental in temporarily changing a state law that ended up being one of the biggest game changers during the pandemic. Any restaurant with a beer, wine, and spirit license was now able to sell alcoholic beverages to go. The only caveat was that any mixed drink sold required the alcohol and the mix to be served separately. Although the industry was grateful for this change in the law, it did not go far enough.

The TRA pleaded with lawmakers to allow restaurants to sell their customers a completely mixed cocktail. They finally agreed to this a few weeks into the nationwide shutdown. This was a game changer for our industry. Our guests were ordering gallons of margaritas to go. This new law, which was only temporary, helped restaurants survive the pandemic of 2020. The legislators saw the public response and the tax benefit of allowing restaurants to sell alcohol to go, and Governor Greg Abbott made the law permanent.

Every restaurant in Texas benefits from the efforts of the TRA, despite not all of them being members of the organization. It speaks volumes about the reputation of a restaurant owner who only wants to benefit from the TRA yet does not make the necessary investment by paying membership dues and making a small contribution to the Texas Restaurant Association's Political Action Committee.

Not only have I chaired this committee in the past, but I have been its number-one contributor for the last ten years. I would never ask another restaurateur to do something I'm not willing to do myself. If you own a restaurant in Texas and are not a Texas Restaurant Association member, please consider joining today. The networking is invaluable, and it alone is worth the annual membership dues.

The Texas Restaurant Association's website, https://www.tx restaurant.org, is a resource center where restaurateurs can tap into a vast amount of information that will enhance their efficiency and profitability.

Now, with as many lawmakers as there are in the great state of Texas looking for the next easy target by which to raise revenues for a cash-strapped state—not to mention the hundreds of lawyers hovering over businesses, ready to devour them—I can assure you that if there were no association representing the food service industry, we all would be paying many times more in fees and taxes than what your membership dues would be.

Oh, did I mention the added benefit of networking with other operators and tapping into their years of restaurant experience? How about the investments into our future food service associates through our local chapter (Greater Houston Texas Restaurant Association) scholarship programs? During the pandemic, the TRA went to bat for us and won the privilege to serve alcohol to go. This win alone saved many restaurants from going out of business.

If you are a restaurant owner and not in Texas, join your state's association. And if you are not in the restaurant industry, then join your local industry association. If your local or state trade association isn't doing a good job, get in there and help! If there isn't an association, start one!

Remember, the whole is greater than the sum of our parts.

BUILD PEOPLE RELATIONSHIPS

One of the most important lessons I learned when I worked for my dad at El Toro Restaurants in the early '80s was how important public relations is to a business's reputation. The term *public relations* is another way of describing *people relationships*. At the end of the day, for any business to be successful, it must develop and maintain meaningful relationships with people. I often tell our staff we are in the people business. We just happen to sell Tex-Mex.

Yes, I do realize that social media isn't going anywhere anytime soon, and it does play a vital role in our society. However, I can guarantee nothing more solid or more satisfying than a real person-to-person relationship. This is something Facebook, Instagram, and X (formerly known as Twitter) simply cannot deliver.

While I was handling accounts payable for El Toro, one particular invoice would land on my desk from a company called Ted Roggen Advertising and Public Relations. I never enjoyed cutting the check for this service because I could not see the value in it. Each time I received an invoice from Ted Roggen's firm, I would present it to my dad and ask him to consider canceling the service. My dad's response was always the same: "Pay it!"

Ted Roggen spent almost two years as a prisoner of war during World War II before resuming civilian life in 1945, when he started his firm in Houston. Some of Ted's early clients included Liberace, the Supremes, Judy Garland, Louis Armstrong, and Ray Charles. Ted was also instrumental in assisting Ninfa Laurenzo with the launch of the Original Ninfas. Ninfa Laurenzo was a beloved Houston restaurateur known for introducing fajitas to the Mexican restaurant scene back in 1973 at her ten-table restaurant just east of downtown Houston.

My dad hired Ted in 1961, shortly after he opened his first

restaurant in La Porte. Ted provided various PR services, including billboards, newspaper ads, and announcements in the Movers and Shakers column of the *Houston Chronicle* and the *Houston Post*. Monica and I even had our wedding announcement make it to the pages of both Houston newspapers.

A few years ago, I decided to give Ted a call to see how he was doing. I must admit, my heart sank when I heard that familiar sound: "We're sorry, but the number you have dialed is no longer in service. Please check your number and dial again." After all, if Ted had been alive at the time, he would have been ninety-six years old. After a little research, I discovered that Ted's firm had a website that listed two phone numbers. I called the first one but got no answer. Then, I called the second number, which turned out to be his home office number.

In a very quiet voice, a man answered, "Hello?"

I said, "Ted, is this you?"

"Yes, this is Ted."

I cannot tell you how pleasantly surprised I was to hear his voice on the other end of the line. We spoke briefly about everything from his daily routine to his wife winning her battle with cancer. Ted told me that he exercises every day and watches what he eats. His wife, Sid, keeps the butter away from him, but he still manages to sneak some from time to time when she's not watching.

In an interview with the *Houston Chronicle* in 2011, Ted was asked how the public relations business has changed over the years. His response:

The main thing is the computer. It makes it easier. But it's not the answer. You still have to be visible. You have to look at the client eyeball to eyeball. I still drive the freeways and call on clients, even though I don't like driving the freeways—it's treacherous.[13]

Ted passed away from old age in 2022. He was 104 years old. I'm happy that I kept in touch with Ted over the last several years. And it wasn't until more recently that I fully understood why my dad insisted on my paying those Ted Roggen invoices back in the '80s. Ted gave my dad something very special, something every young person in business needs to succeed. He gave my dad the confidence he needed to continue operating a business despite the challenges that were in front of him.

And in some ways, that confidence has been passed down to me, and I'm grateful for it.

I must admit, when I worked for my dad, I did not understand his reasoning for using Ted Roggen's firm, but ask me now, and I could easily tell you. It's the relationship you have with people that makes the difference. All of business and all of life is about relationships!

How the public views your company is extremely important

---

13 David Kaplan, "PR Man Roggen Still Talks Up Clients at Age 93," *Houston Chronicle*, August 13, 2011, https://www.chron.com/business/article/pr-man-roggen-still-talks-up-clients-at-age-93-1935985.php/.

and will actually determine your brand. You cannot leave that to chance. Having a person like Ted to manage that for you is critical.

In today's world, having a timely, positive response to any social media post about your company is equally critical, whether the criticism or complaint is legitimate or not.

Your ability to respond with a positive instead of a negative attitude will help you build the right kind of relationship with the community and, therefore, glean a stronger reputation of character in the marketplace.

In other words, your ability to respond positively instead of being offended and reacting negatively is a powerful habit. Today, people seem to be so easily offended, which can cause you to do the same if you aren't careful.

This is true in any relationship, not just guest relations. Your responsibility toward team members, vendors, and even your family to own your mistakes and respond appropriately to their actions is vital to success. If you do not own up to your actions, you will reap the consequences.

BENEFITS OF A GOOD REPUTATION

In 2005, I was selected by a local chamber of commerce to be one of only four individuals to participate in a Town Hall meeting with President George W. Bush in Washington, D.C. We were there to discuss his Social Security reform bill. We were seated at a large table on a stage with an audience of about four hundred people. Every time the president spoke or looked in my direction, a mass of camera shutters clicked. It was a surreal feeling to witness this. As I sat on that stage next to the man who held the highest office in our country and arguably the most powerful position on Earth, I experienced every emotion one would expect in that situation.

"How did I get here?" I wondered. I thought about the journey from the "open" sign to the life I am blessed to lead today and the team I am blessed to lead. It was very similar to the feeling I got when that first guest walked into that very first location.

I never, ever want to lose that feeling.

Success has a funny way of distorting your self-esteem. It allows you to see life from a totally different lens and tempts you to think that you are the reason for your success. That is only *partly* true. If not for my wonderful team and loyal guests, I would not be where I am today.

The habit of guarding your reputation has many benefits. The favor and trust that you cultivate from others can be remarkable. On this day, not only did I find myself sharing the stage with the sitting president of the United States, contributing my experience for the benefit of our country, but I even got a "First Endorsement." President Bush told those back in Houston watching C-SPAN to "go eat at Russell's restaurant"!

The one fact that I try to instill in my children is that during their lifetime, they will never truly own a single tangible object. As a matter of fact, all they will ever have is the opportunity to manage "things." Depending on how well they do it, this will ultimately determine how many more "things" they get to manage during their lifetime. That being said, there is one thing that they will own, and only they will be able to determine its value—and that is their reputation.

To-Go Items

1. Your reputation is the most valuable thing you will ever own because you are the only one in control of it.

2. Protect your reputation by never having it questioned.

3. When you do mess up, the important thing is how you respond.

4. A business's reputation will always be more valuable than any dollar amount that may be in dispute.

5. Build meaningful relationships that are developed on candor, honesty, mutual respect, and integrity.

CHAPTER 4

Develop the Habit of Giving

~~~~~~

We must rise above the narrow confines of our
individualistic concerns with a broader concern
for all humanity.

—MARTIN LUTHER KING JR., "Birth of a New Age"

I f there is one thing that I know for certain, it is this: There
is something very powerful in giving. When a person gives
something of value to another person, especially in a time of
need, it has a more profound effect on the giver than it does on
the receiver. Furthermore, businesses that give to their employees and the community that supports them gain a competitive

advantage over their competitors. People will gravitate to a giver, especially to one who gives for the sake of giving, expecting absolutely nothing in return.

Growing up as a young child, I witnessed my parents always helping others in different ways. My father would always support Little League sports by sponsoring teams. One year after the team won the championship, he treated the entire team to dinner at the El Toro Restaurant in La Porte. Another year, my father helped the mayor raise money so the police department could provide a bulletproof vest to every police officer in La Porte. In 1977, my father purchased the very first grand champion steer at the La Porte Livestock Show and Rodeo. My parents also helped several families from Mexico go through the immigration process to become naturalized U.S. citizens. Seeing them both always doing for others made such a huge impression on me, and I hope my children and grandchildren continue this habit of always wanting to help others. What I hope they discover, as I have, is that there is no better feeling in life than seeing the impact your actions can have on others.

A PURPOSE BEYOND PROFIT

I love what Ed Freeman, a professor at the University of Virginia Darden School of Business and a leader in the Conscious Capitalism movement, had to say regarding profits: "We need red blood cells to live (the same way a business needs profits to live), but the purpose of life is more than to make red blood cells (the same way the purpose of business is more than simply to generate profits)."[14]

Profits are important so we can live out our purpose. The consumer helps create the world it wants to see through the businesses it chooses to support. A person can help their community grow and prosper simply by choosing to patronize businesses that give back to the community. There's nothing wrong with a business owner living an abundant lifestyle so long as it's on par with how they give back. Imagine for a moment that one of our long-time customers reaches out to us and asks for a gift card to help out with their child's school fundraiser and, for whatever reason, is told no. Now, if this same person drives across town to one of our competitors and asks them for the same donation, and they agree to give it, you can almost guess what restaurant this parent will visit the next time the family dines, no matter which restaurant has the best food. Having delicious food is important, but not nearly as important as expressing gratitude for a customer's longtime support of their establishment. Supporting a community is much more than just the act of giving itself; it is the best way a business can say thank you.

When it comes to supporting local charitable causes, most businesses will pay attention to what their competitors are doing. It's the peer pressure alone that forces many companies to do at least what their competition is doing. Many small businesses are

---

14 Quoted in Conscious Capitalism, "About Conscious Capitalism," accessed November 9, 2023, https://europeanconference.consciouscapitalism.org/about-cc/.

not in a position to give as much as others, and that's fine. But they should be willing to give according to their ability. Giving isn't something a business does once it becomes big or successful. It is something that should be a part of its DNA from the beginning so that one day, it can give even more. Social media is a great vehicle for a business to show the community all the various nonprofits it supports. For over the past twenty years, the Original Gringo's location in Pearland has donated the opening inventory to the Little League Baseball concession stand, a donation value of $7,500 each year.

PRACTICE EMPATHY AND GENEROSITY

Empathy is defined as the understanding of our shared humanity. It's the ability to see yourself in another person's shoes. Compassionate empathy goes beyond simply understanding others and sharing their feelings; it actually moves us to take action to help another person in need however we can with whatever we have. Giving isn't so much about how much a person can give to help someone as it is the act itself. Whenever a person receives a gift during a low point in their life, what they're really experiencing is someone actually caring about them enough to help them. What they receive has little to do with what it was versus who it was that did it.

As mentioned earlier, I'm extremely fortunate to have witnessed the many acts of generosity my parents did for others. One of them was seeing my parents load up a cargo van full of clothes and Spanish-language Bibles and drive over a thousand miles to Atacheo, a small town deep in the interior of Mexico, to deliver them to rural, economically disadvantaged communities. This single act alone had a profound effect on me, and I have been blessed with the opportunity to continue my parents' legacy of compassionate empathy.

One such opportunity came in the wake of Hurricane Katrina, which devastated the Gulf Coast states, including the city of New Orleans, in August 2005. The flooding in New Orleans happened so quickly that it forced many residents to flee the city with very little time to spare. It was the costliest storm on record until Hurricane Harvey in 2017.

The impact of this storm would force many evacuees to make Houston their new home. Knowing that many of them would need help getting established in their new city, I knew Gringo's would do its small part to help ease their pain.

My cousin Rick Noriega, a former Texas State Representative and an officer in the Texas Army National Guard, returned home from his tour in Afghanistan and was appointed by Houston's mayor, Bill White, to oversee the evacuees sheltering at the George R. Brown Convention Center. At one time, as many as 9,000 evacuees were taking refuge inside the convention center because they had nowhere else to go.

I visited Rick at the evacuee center one Sunday afternoon to see what this effort looked like. I wanted to get an appreciation for how much work goes into providing shelter to that many people. While he was giving me a tour, I was blown away by the sheer number of volunteers that were required to help assist so many displaced people. The entire convention center floor was covered with inflatable mattresses and cots.

As I was leaving the convention center and walking to my car, I noticed from a distance that a small group of people were standing directly behind my car. As I got closer, I also noticed that they had several black trash bags filled with clothes lying on the ground directly behind my car. When they noticed that it was my car they were blocking, they quickly apologized and rushed to move the bags. I told them not to worry and to take their time. I began conversing with Alvin Lee, who was there with his aunt, grandfather, and other relatives. He told me that the water in New Orleans rose so quickly that they had almost no time to do anything except throw a bunch of their clothes inside trash bags and hop on a bus to get away from the city as fast as they could.

As I was driving home after leaving the convention center, I kept thinking about this family and their situation. We had exchanged phone numbers, and I'm glad we did. Since our company's plan was to help the victims of this storm in some way, I figured that we would help this family get back on their feet and make them feel welcome in Houston. I called Alvin to let him know that Gringo's would be adopting their family.

One of the very first things we did was purchase a new Chevrolet Malibu for them. Next, we rented a house, completely furnished it with new furniture, paid their utilities for an entire year, and also gave them a monthly grocery allowance. This family was now in a position to restart their lives.

I've stayed in touch with Alvin over the years. It turns out that he was a star athlete in high school, and since Hurricane Katrina, he's been on two VH1 reality shows. (As an aside, his aunt was a taste tester for the Zatarain's Spice Company. As a restaurateur, I think it is very cool.)

They say that coincidence is God's way of remaining anonymous. Well, I do know that was true for this family anyway. Placing their bags directly behind my car was not an accident. God had to have had His hand on them, especially when you think about the fact that there were hundreds of vehicles in the parking lot that day. I'm sure the Lee family thinks about that day often and how one random stranger's act of kindness helped change their trajectory during one of the most difficult times in their lives.

A VITAL CAUSE

I consider myself extremely fortunate to have the freedom to own and operate a business in this great country. I wouldn't be able to live out this dream if it weren't for the brave men and women who serve in our armed forces. Unfortunately, far too many of them return home after being honorably discharged, and they suffer a different kind of wound, an unseen one called post-traumatic stress.

As I learned more about the impact post-traumatic stress disorder (PTSD) and other mental illnesses have on military veterans, I wanted to find a way to help. Since 2001, America has lost more than 125,000 veterans to suicide.[15] In 2020, that was 16.8 veterans every day.[16] The PTSD Foundation estimates an even higher number, at forty-four veterans per day.[17] This is a serious, serious crisis. And it's unacceptable.

Then, in 2014, my friend and radio talk show host Michael Berry approached me about joining the Camp Hope board of directors. He was serving as the national spokesperson for the organization at the time. Camp Hope is a program run by the nonprofit organization PTSD Foundation of America that provides interim housing for combat veterans who have combat-related PTSD. Founded in May 2012 by businessman Gene Birdwell of Birdwell Construction, Camp Hope is run by an incredible and dedicated staff. Executive director David Maulsby, president Dr. Ryan Rodgers, and their team of counselors and volunteers do an outstanding job of creating a sanctuary for any veteran in need of help. Camp Hope's staff is a unique team of combat veterans and pastoral staff who are trained to work with victims of trauma and PTSD in a caring and positive environment.

Joining the board was a no-brainer.

Once I got involved with Camp Hope, one of the first things

---

15 Stop Soldier Suicide, "Veteran Suicide," accessed February 20, 2024, https://stopsoldiersuicide.org/vet-stats.

16 U.S. Department of Veterans Affairs, "National Veteran Suicide Prevention Annual Report," September 2022, https://www.mentalhealth.va.gov/docs/data-sheets/2022/2022-National-Veteran-Suicide-Prevention-Annual-Report-FINAL-508.pdf.

17 PTSD Foundation of America, "About PTSD Foundation of America," accessed November 9, 2023, https://ptsdusa.org/about/.

I noticed was that the residents didn't have a real gym to work out in. What they did have inside the mess hall was a very small, closet-like area filled with a lot of donated home gym equipment. I asked whether space for a new gym could be allocated inside a new building being constructed next door to the mess hall, and the board of directors approved it.

There's a saying I once heard: "If you want something done quickly, then find the busiest person you know, and they'll get it done!"

Jonathan Kim, Gringo's chief operating officer at the time, gave his time to help by reaching out to our vendors Sysco, U.S. Foods, Ben E. Keith, Houston Avocado, Martin Food Service, and a few others, asking them to consider making a small contribution to the gym project at Camp Hope. Within just a few hours, Jonathan was able to raise more than $60,000 to equip the new gym with all-new Cybex equipment.

During a barbecue cook-off fundraiser at Camp Hope, we held a ribbon-cutting ceremony in front of the gym and surprised Jonathan by unveiling the name, the Jonathan Kim Gym.

In December 2017, Jonathan and I were at the office talking about a book I had just finished reading called *Living with a Seal* by Jesse Itzler, owner of the Atlanta Hawks and husband of Sara Blakely, the founder of Spanx. The Seal turned out to be an ultra-marathoner by the name of David Goggins, hired by Jesse to train him like a Navy SEAL for thirty-one days. In 2013, Goggins set a Guinness World Record when he completed 4,030 pull-ups in seventeen hours. Because Jonathan works out regularly and is always up for a challenge, I asked him how many pull-ups he thought he could do in a day.

While he was thinking about it, I mentioned that such a challenge could make a good fundraiser for Camp Hope. Jonathan was all in. We called it Pull-Ups for a Purpose. Jonathan reached out to friends and family, business associates, and our vendors, who all contributed a dollar amount to this campaign. Donation amounts were anywhere from $100 to $10,000 and were guaranteed regardless of whether he completed the 2,000 pull-ups or not. Jonathan decided his goal would be to complete 2,000 pull-ups, and he would do it on Memorial Day 2018 inside the Jonathan Kim Gym at Camp Hope.

Starting in January 2018, Jonathan began his training, both physically and mentally, to prepare himself for this incredible feat. His training over the next five months was like watching a madman on a mission; his workouts lasted hours.

Then came Memorial Day. Jonathan and his support team, led by Gringo's senior VP John Fernandez, arrived at Camp Hope early in the morning to begin the ten-plus-hour Pull-Ups for a Purpose challenge. His plan consisted of four pull-ups per minute for sixty minutes straight, rest for fifteen minutes, and then repeat. The veterans at Camp Hope were there to witness this incredible feat, and as the day went on, more and more people gathered to watch. Things were going according to plan until pull-up number six hundred, when Jonathan started to feel symptoms of dehydration, causing his muscles to cramp up. He was so determined to finish what he started that he was not going to let that stop him. Between each set, he would have to apply ice and have his arms massaged.

The fatigue Jonathan was experiencing was very obvious toward the end of his challenge. Everyone in the room could tell that he was in severe pain. At around pull-up number 1,842, I made the decision to step in and tell Jonathan that he did it, that he had accomplished the challenge, and that it was okay to stop. Never before in my life had I witnessed someone so determined to finish what they set out to do and who was not going to quit, no matter what. Jonathan could have easily been a Navy SEAL.

Jonathan was disappointed that he didn't complete his goal of 2,000 pull-ups. Several of the residents at Camp Hope were so impressed by what Jonathan had just done for them that without a word being spoken, several veterans stepped up and took turns finishing the remaining 158 pull-ups, reaching Jonathan's goal of 2,000. When Jonathan saw what the veterans had just done, it gave him the strength to do one more to complete the challenge at 2,001 pull-ups. Everyone in attendance that day who witnessed this incredible exhibition of grit and determination was so touched that there was not a dry eye in the house.

Jonathan's effort raised over $106,000 for Camp Hope and, more importantly, brought awareness to our community that help is available for veterans who have PTSD. I promised Jonathan that I would never challenge him to perform another insane feat again because I knew if I did, he would do it, especially if it would help our veterans.

At Gringo's and Jimmy Changas, we also created a special

Tex-Mex combination plate that is permanently on our menu, with two dollars from each portion sold going directly to Camp Hope. As of 2023, we've raised well over a million dollars and counting from this one dish alone, thanks to our loyal customers.

As I mention in the introduction, the profits from this book go directly to Camp Hope, so everyone who purchases this book becomes part of Camp Hope's mission.

If you want to give your life meaning and purpose beyond the world of stuff—if you want to find a place in your life where you will discover the only thing that can give you true inner peace—then find a cause, like the PTSD Foundation of America and Camp Hope, that enriches the lives of your fellow human beings.

Enriching the lives of others is the most noble and worthy journey a human being can be on.

If you are a veteran or know a veteran who's exhibiting symptoms of PTSD, please call Camp Hope's 24-hour hotline, 1-877-717-PTSD.

THE TORO ROOM

I first got to know Leroy Sandoval Jr. in the early 1990s when he was a seventh grader at a private Christian school in Pasadena, Texas, where my wife, Monica, was a kindergarten teacher. Leroy's mother, Zaida, was her teacher's assistant. I had learned that Leroy's parents had recently divorced, leaving Zaida to raise Leroy and his younger sister Amy all on her own. When Leroy's parents divorced, he had a difficult time dealing with it. He just couldn't understand why his dad had left his mom.

On occasion, Monica would share their family's situation with me and the financial hardship caused by the divorce. So I decided that I would help their family financially. From the time Leroy was in junior high until he graduated from high school, I sent Monica an envelope each month containing $200 to help out the Sandoval family. It wasn't a lot of money, but at the time I started doing this, I was operating only a single restaurant, and money could be tight.

Every month, I would write Leroy's name on the envelope, and below it, I would include the words "Man of the House." I wanted Leroy to understand the significance that his role played as the only male in the house and in his family's future. Leroy probably didn't understand why I was helping his family, but my gesture must have had a positive impact on him because he promised his mom that when he grew up, he was going to take care of her.

After Leroy graduated from high school, he worked a number of different day jobs before he decided to join the Marines. Boot camp was especially difficult for Leroy because of his smaller stature, but he persevered and became a Marine in the fall of 2003. That December, shortly before his first deployment to Iraq, Leroy contacted me. He asked if he and his sister Amy could take me out to lunch at the Olive Garden near our house.

During our lunch, Leroy thanked me for the many years of financial support. I remember thanking Leroy for his service to our country, and I let him know I was proud of him. I also told Leroy that once he returned from his first deployment, he and I would set a plan to go out and have a nice steak dinner to celebrate.

When we arrived back at my house after having lunch, I told

Leroy and his sister to wait for me outside in his pickup truck while I ran inside the house to grab their Christmas gifts. I put together a couple of cards and included a nice check in each. As Leroy and his sister drove off, I remember watching them from my home office window. Both of them were smiling from ear to ear as they drove away.

I didn't know it at the time, but that would be the last time that I saw Leroy alive. Pfc. Leroy Sandoval Jr. was killed in action on March 26, 2004, while on a tour in Fallujah, Afghanistan, during Operation Iraqi Freedom. Leroy was a machine gunner from the battalion's Fox Company and was known as "Smokey" to the other members of his platoon.

He was only twenty-one years old.

In June 2004, our company completed construction of the new Original Gringo's building in Pearland. On the Fourth of July, we held a ceremony to dedicate the building in Leroy's honor. One of the four dining rooms at the new Original Gringo's is called the Toro Room because of the five bull heads that hang throughout the dining room. Before we reopened the new building, we had to return one of the bull heads because it had a defect. The day we received the replacement was the same day we dedicated the building in Leroy's honor.

Most of the bull heads that come in from Mexico have a plaque attached to them with information pertaining to that particular bull head, including the name of the bull, the weight, the ranch where it was raised, and the name of the matador who won the fight.

The name of the bull that we received the day we dedicated

the new building in honor of Leroy was Soldado. In English, it means soldier.

Leroy's promise to take care of his mother was more than just a childhood dream. Shortly after his death, Zaida started receiving life insurance checks in the mail. At first, Zaida had a difficult time accepting these checks because she felt uncomfortable receiving money from Leroy after his death. So she decided to invest the money with our company and has been receiving interest payments for the last eighteen-plus years. Leroy's promise to take care of his mother ended up being very prophetic.

I sincerely thank Leroy and every person who has ever served our country in the military. America is fortunate to have so many brave men and women who voluntarily serve in our armed forces. Every American owes them a debt of gratitude that can never entirely be repaid.

To-Go Items

1. Give, and it will be given back to you.

2. Giving isn't so much about how much a person can give to help someone as the act itself.

3. Enriching the lives of others is the noblest journey you can go on.

CHAPTER 5

Surround Yourself with People Who Make You Better

~~~~~~

As iron sharpens iron, so one person sharpens another.

—PROVERBS 27:17 (NIV)

I f you've ever put a jigsaw puzzle together, then you realize that, even though you already know what the final outcome should look like, it still requires you to search for the correct piece of the puzzle to complete the picture.

Starting a business from scratch is not much different, except that while you're attempting to build your business, you have to constantly look over your shoulder to make sure your competition is not catching up, maneuver through government laws and regulations, and be aware of potential lawsuits.

When Gringo's opened for business on January 11, 1993, the picture of what I wanted it to become was merely in my imagination. Survival, obviously, was the first thing on my agenda. But, as each month passed, there were signs (like being able to pay our vendors and make payroll) that we just might make it.

That's when I began to visualize the company's future. There were a few restaurants I admired for various reasons, and I wanted to emulate ideas from each of them at Gringo's. Whether it was the overall organization and systems of a particular chain or a certain architectural look or interior design of another when I saw something we could use that would help us become better, I would make an effort to go after it.

As I began to put the pieces together for Gringo's, it was important that I understood my strengths and weaknesses. Every business owner must have enough self-awareness to understand what they are good at and what they are not. Many seem to overlook this all-important fact.

If you have a dream, you need a team. The bigger the dream, the stronger the team needs to be. Each puzzle piece was strategically placed so our company could continue to the next level. The most important pieces are our people, of course.

If you are going to scale your company, your executive leadership team is key.

I learned this lesson as a young adult working for El Toro. There, I was fortunate to cross paths with a number of talented individuals whose passion for their business made a huge impression on me. One of those persons was Juan Martinez, a.k.a. "Mr. John." Mr. John was the executive chef for El Toro Restaurants. My father hired Mr. John a couple of years after opening his first restaurant in the early '60s. Mr. John was directly responsible for developing every single one of the El Toro recipes, some of which serve as models for recipes at Gringo's and Jimmy Changas.

Mr. John had a keen palate as well as a desire to use only the highest-quality ingredients available. His duties included purchasing ingredients for the El Toro commissary, or central kitchen, and he would select the most expensive cheeses for their enchiladas and chile con queso, as well as the best cooking oil that Kraft Foodservice offered at the time.

Mr. John believed in processing everything from scratch at the El Toro central kitchen in Baytown. Some of the items the kitchen prepared for the restaurants included hot sauce, refried beans, beef picadillo, chile con queso, and enchilada gravy, for which Mr. John would only use the Gebhardt brand chili powder. He was also a master at large batch cooking, using two sixty-gallon Groen steam kettles to process most items. He believed that El Toro should grind its own beef for the taco meat, cut its own steaks, and make tamales every Saturday morning.

I can remember, as a twelve-year-old kid, going with my father to the central kitchen on Saturday mornings to help make tamales so I could earn some spending money for the week. I'd always work approximately five hours and was paid the federal minimum wage of $2.10 per hour. I can also remember calculating in my mind as I was pulling the fresh tamales off the conveyor how much pay I would receive at the end of the shift.

After graduating from high school, I went to work at the El Toro in La Porte, where I earned my MBA (mop bucket attendant). Then, in the early '80s, when the Houston economy was struggling, I convinced my father and Mr. John to begin buying lower-priced, lower-quality ingredients in an attempt to try and save the company money. This ended up being a huge mistake, and the effects were felt almost immediately, with an increase in guest complaints and declining sales. We obviously had to go back to purchasing the higher-quality and more expensive ingredients—which remains my philosophy to this day.

Mr. John's protégé, Hugo Olvera, a.k.a. Dos Caballos (because he does the work of two men), has served as another inspiration to me. Hugo is one of the hardest-working individuals I have ever met. I had the privilege of working with Hugo for a brief period in the mid-1980s at the El Toro on Decker Drive in Baytown, so I was already familiar with his work ethic. I describe in Chapter 3 how punctual he is, but loyal, honest, and dependable are just a few of the other words Hugo embodies. When I made the decision to open the first Gringo's in Pearland in 1993, I knew that the first and probably most important person I needed to hire was Hugo as my executive chef. Although he was not a formally trained chef, he knew how to cook Tex-Mex. And he was the first piece of the puzzle.

Mr. John passed away in 1983. Although he is no longer

with us, his legacy continues through Hugo. When someone is eating in our restaurants, they are enjoying the passion for high-quality, great-tasting food that has been passed down from my father's time.

Mr. John and Hugo both exemplify why it's important to surround yourself with people who make you better. They helped make El Toro better for many years, and their legacy has continued with Gringo's. I also learned to recognize when I needed to bring in people to complement my own strengths and to handle those things I wasn't an expert in.

That can include people who don't work directly for me at Gringo's but are still vital to our success. Shortly after opening the first Gringo's in January 1993, I realized that owning only one restaurant was not going to get me where I wanted to go in life. So, almost immediately, I began searching for my second location. When I decided La Porte was where I would build next, I knew exactly who I wanted to design the building, and that person was architect Davis Wilson.

Davis, a proud Marine, is an older gentleman who enjoys smoking a pipe when meeting with clients. Davis attended the University of Houston in the early '70s, where he earned his degree in architecture. He is extremely talented and has the natural ability to create some incredible concept sketches.

As a matter of fact, one of Davis's earliest jobs was as a caricature artist at Astroworld (a theme park next to Houston's Astrodome complex) when it first opened in 1968. Some of Davis's earliest clients included Tilman Fertitta, for whom he designed the

Landry's Seafood Restaurant. He also designed buildings for my siblings' restaurants, Johnny Tamales in Pasadena and El Toro on Garth Road in Baytown.

I had never built a restaurant from the ground up before, so I was very dependent on Davis's expertise when it came to the various facets of real estate development—from meeting with city planners and understanding what a G702 payment application form was to knowing how real estate covenants affect your overall development. Davis's mind is an encyclopedia of so much useful information when it comes to development that I wish there were a way I could transfer all that information to my brain.

MY SENIOR EXECUTIVE TEAM

I've been very fortunate over the years to have attracted some of the best talents to come to work with me. The following are some of those individuals who have helped Gringo's become a company that I am so very proud of. Each one of them has played a significant role, and I can honestly say neither Gringo's Tex-Mex nor Jimmy Changas would be here today (or at least not in their current form) had it not been for these team members. My senior leadership team consists of John Fernandez, Danny Hanks, Heather McKeon, and Jonathan Kim. They have been with the company for an average of twenty-five years. Each one of them could easily run the company with the same passion and commitment to excellence that I do.

John Fernandez, Senior VP of Operations

I first met John Fernandez shortly after I opened the first Gringo's in 1993. He lived a couple of streets over and would often visit the restaurant along with his younger brother, Rick. The moment I met John, I immediately knew that his personality was exactly the kind I needed to help me run the front-of-the-house operations. John was familiar with this building because, at the age of fourteen, he had worked in it when it was an El Toro. What attracted me to John was his personality. I knew if I could convince him to join me, he would be able to deliver hospitality. He is a natural at making a customer feel welcome. Since John was already a huge fan of Gringo's, I asked him to consider coming to work for me. It was obviously a huge gamble for him since, at the time, we were only a single-unit operation.

When John agreed to join Gringo's, he had only one request—he wanted to finish college at the University of Houston, which he did. John joined us in June 1995 as general manager. John's passion for excellence and enthusiasm for people have been very instrumental in helping build the culture at Gringo's. John's faith and kindness of heart have touched generations of our customers and team members. He has the qualities of a mentor. As the general manager of that location for a decade, John's enthusiasm to motivate the staff to excellence was something to witness and continues to this day. He joined our executive team in 2007 when Danny Hanks assumed the GM role. Since 1995, the Original Gringo's has had only four general managers: John Fernandez, Danny Hanks, Matt Bussa, and the current GM, Hugo Espinosa.

I appreciate John more than he will ever know. I've told him on several occasions that had he not joined me twenty-eight years ago, Gringo's might still be around, but it would not be the same company that it is today.

Danny Hanks, Chief Procurement Officer

Danny Hanks joined Gringo's in La Porte as a young server in February 1998. Because of Danny's incredible work ethic, he moved up quickly through the ranks to become assistant manager and then general manager. And then, in 2005, Danny was promoted to general manager of our flagship location, the Original Gringo's in Pearland. Danny created a standard of excellence that all our GMs have aspired to emulate.

Danny was born into a family of firefighters who served their community with honor and dignity, and his parents instilled in him the values of faith and hard work. His decision to not follow his family's tradition of firefighting was our company's gain.

Today, after twenty-five years in operations, Danny is our chief procurement officer. Danny is in charge of procuring almost every single item we purchase from our two primary distributors, Ben E. Keith and U.S. Foods. Danny's main focus is to make sure we are receiving the best pricing possible based on our purchasing volume. He possesses a special kind of energy and commitment that every employer wishes their entire team had.

Heather McKeon, Chief Operating Officer

Heather joined us as a hostess shortly after we opened the Gringo's in La Porte in October 1996. By 2000, I was looking for someone to head up marketing at our new corporate offices in La Porte when Joel Perkins, my franchise partner who'd just opened the Fuqua location, mentioned to me that Heather had finished her marketing degree and would be excellent for this new position. I asked Heather to consider the position, and she accepted.

This move created a new level of talent and momentum for our corporate team. Our company is extremely fortunate to have Heather. She is one of the best multitaskers I have ever witnessed. She is so passionate about our brands that I'm sure a lot of people probably see her face before mine whenever Gringo's comes up in a conversation.

In January 2024, Heather was appointed chief operating officer. I rely on Heather tremendously, and she always delivers excellence. She is constantly educating herself and always trying to be a student of business. She is not shy about being candid and leads the company by example. And if that's not enough, she wears too many hats to count, including event planner and travel agent. Her ability to create fun and excitement everywhere she goes is a joy to watch.

Jonathan Kim, President

Jonathan Kim joined our team in June 2000 as general manager of the Gringo's in La Porte. I quickly saw outstanding qualities in

Jonathan; he was energetic and never met a stranger. I instantly felt a great working relationship with him, and it wasn't long before he became my chief operating officer and right-hand man. I could not have the peace of mind that I have running this company if he wasn't by my side. Eventually, he was promoted to COO.

His ethics and candor make him highly respected by everyone who works with him. He has a remarkable ability to have the pulse of the company at all times, and anytime I have a question regarding just about anything going on in the company, all I have to do is send Jonathan a text message or email, and I'll get an answer within minutes, sometimes seconds. Our company is successful for many reasons, but I can assure you that we are where we are because of Jonathan's commitment to this company and its people. In January 2024, Jonathan was appointed president.

I am so proud of my executive team. I could not have the peace of mind that I do if it were not for them by my side. We truly are greater as a whole than the sum of our parts when it comes to the success of our company. All of them have given the company what I call the prime years of their life—and it does not go unnoticed by me. I appreciate each one of them more than they will ever know.

A VALUED PARTNERSHIP

Another person who has made a significant impact on my life and success is my past franchise partner and close friend, Joel Perkins. I firmly believe that if you want to be the best at something, then you must go out and find the best who are already doing it and mimic them while simultaneously applying your techniques. Fortunately for me, in this situation, I didn't have to go very far to find one of the best restaurant chains in America, located right here in Houston—Pappas Restaurants.

Because I have always admired Pappas's high level of standards and operations, I always told myself if I had any chance of being anything like them as a restaurant operator, I had two choices. One, work for them and learn everything I possibly could, or two, hire someone who worked for them.

I chose the latter.

In the early '90s, my wife, Monica, was a kindergarten teacher at Faith Christian Academy in Pasadena. One of her students, Lindsey Perkins, was very proud of her daddy and where he worked. She would go to class and, on occasion, announce to Monica that her daddy was the general manager of Pappasito's Cantina located in Webster. (Pappasito's is one of the most successful and well-known Tex-Mex restaurants in the Houston area, started by the Pappas family in 1983.) So, of course, Monica would come home and remind me that her student's father was the GM of Pappasito's. I stored this in the back of my mind.

When the development of the second Gringo's in La Porte began in 1995, I discovered that Joel was no longer with Pappasito's, and he had moved on to help open the new Kemah Cantina, now operating as the Aquarium Restaurant, which is owned by Landry's Inc. My family's tortilla company, El Matador, just so happened to sell tortillas to the Kemah Cantina. As the new Gringo's location was getting closer to completion, I asked my cousin Chuck Rivera, who worked for El Matador, to pass on to Joel that I was looking for a GM to help me open the new Gringo's.

Joel contacted me almost immediately, and we met several times over the next five months. Truth be told, I would have hired him after the first interview, but I did not have the money to pay him. Keep in mind, in early 1995, I only had the one Gringo's location in Pearland. I continued to meet with Joel while at the same time delaying a job offer until we were closer to opening. Joel joined the Gringo's team in May 1996.

What I did not know when I was interviewing Joel was that he did not want to leave Pappasito's when he did. He parted ways because he had been demoted from GM, relocated to another location on the north side of town, and his salary was cut by 60 percent. To compound his dire financial situation, his wife, Jamie, was no longer working as an executive secretary, and their fourth daughter, Shelby, had just been born. Had I known this, I probably would have figured out a way to hire him sooner.

Joel helped me open that location on July 1, 1996, and in assembling his team, he hired several incredible team members who are still a part of Gringo's family today. Practically, my entire senior executive team came from that restaurant!

Joel went on to help me open our third Gringo's in Texas City on August 5, 1999, and a few months later, I afforded him the opportunity to franchise his own Gringo's. In early 2000, my cousin Chuck learned that the owner of My Amigos restaurant, Jesse DeLeon, was selling his restaurant on the Gulf Freeway at

Fuqua. That April, Joel and I visited the restaurant as customers on a Thursday night, and business was very slow. As we walked around the restaurant, both of us felt we could easily convert it to a Gringo's at a minimal cost.

On May 1, we finalized a deal with Jesse to purchase his business and assume the lease. I personally financed the entire project for Joel to show my appreciation for him joining our team four years prior. Gringo's Fuqua opened for business on July 24, 2000. It has been one of our best deals ever and also one of our most profitable units.

Back when I was interviewing Joel and putting him off until I could afford to pay him, he must have been getting a little concerned and decided to give me his best line in an attempt to convince me to hire him. He told me, "Russell, if you hire me, I will run that restaurant as if I owned it myself." Those words were very prophetic. After Joel opened Fuqua in 2000, he went on to open four more Gringo's franchise locations: Champions in 2006, Cypress in 2010, Spring in 2013, and the Woodlands in 2018.

In early 2021, Gringo's bought out Joel's five restaurants for eight figures. Joel is now enjoying retirement, but he's also still the landlord on two of those properties, so he'll receive rental income on those for years to come.

LOYALTY, LIVELIHOOD, AND RELATIONSHIPS

One of my favorite stories involves loyalty, livelihood, and relationships—three things that are highly important to me in my life and work. I've been actively involved with the Texas Restaurant Association for many years as a member, director on the board, and committee chair.

Over the course of my involvement with the association, I have developed some great friendships with fellow restaurateurs across the Lone Star State. One of these is with Mark Davis Bailey, past president of the TRA and the owner of several restaurants in the Dallas area called the Original Pancake House. Mark sent me an email in August 2018 asking me if Gringo's was in need of a chief financial officer (CFO). He said that he had the perfect person, a guy by the name of Elio Alfonso. At the time, we already had a full-time CFO—we'll call him Sean—who had taken over the role after Joe Aguilar Jr. passed away in 2012 from health complications.

I didn't know anything about Elio other than Mark saying that he was the best CFO he'd ever worked with. Out of sheer curiosity, I asked Mark to send me some samples of Elio's work. Once I looked them over, I saw immediately that Elio knew his stuff when it came to what restaurant financials should look like. Those financials were the equivalent of what a CFO for a publicly traded company would provide to Wall Street analysts. Not to say anything bad about Sean's work, but for all practical purposes, he had reached his ability for the position he was in, and since we were growing, things needed to change.

The first thing I decided to do was bring Elio on board as a consultant. I wanted to see how well he interacted with the rest of the team in our accounting department. Everything went as planned—and I knew I had to make a big change, removing Sean as our CFO and replacing him with Elio. I wanted to be sensitive to Sean's feelings and to show him the respect he deserved for being on our team since 2005. I am always appreciative to anyone who gives our company some of their most valuable time—their earning years. I did not want to make Sean feel any worse than he was already going to feel by being replaced as the company CFO, so I had to come up with a plan.

I met with Sean on a Monday morning and had my then-COO, Jonathan Kim, join us. It is important always to have a witness sit in on a meeting when the subject matter is highly sensitive. First, I told Sean I had good news and bad news. The good news was that his salary was going to remain the same. The bad news was that he was no longer our CFO, effective the upcoming January 1. I further explained that his new role would be as the full-time buyer for the entire company. Sean's role would go from CFO to senior VP of purchasing, the same position Danny Hanks holds today. This position involves weekly communication with our vendors to secure contract pricing on many of the commodity items we require—everything from the various cheeses we use, the tomatoes for our salsa, outside skirt (the beef we use for our fajitas), packaging material, and many other items. Sean loved the idea. It would free him up from having to make the drive from where he lived in Spring to our corporate offices in La Porte. He could now work from a few of the Gringo's locations closer to his home.

For the next six months, Jonathan and I gave Sean his space

to see how well he could handle the new responsibility as our full-time buyer. After about five months, things were not going as Jonathan and I had hoped. Still being very sensitive to Sean's loyalty for the past fifteen years, I had to make another difficult decision that would affect his future with the company.

I called Sean into the conference room along with Jonathan. The first question I asked Sean was, "Do you trust me?"

"Absolutely, I trust you. I trust you like a father," answered Sean.

I said, "Good. I hope you still feel that way after this meeting."

I immediately followed up with, "Sean, effective immediately, you are no longer with the company."

Obviously, the room got instantly quiet. I quickly shared with Sean that I had a better plan for him that I was almost positive he would like even better than being let go from Gringo's. For starters, I informed him that he would receive six months of severance. And second, we had a job lined up for him that had the potential to double his income. Before our meeting with Sean to cut ties as our CFO, Jonathan had contacted one of our food distributors to inform them that if they considered hiring Sean as our sales representative, Gringo's would, in turn, guarantee them at least 80 percent of our business, which would equate to approximately a $15 million account.

Sean's initial reaction to everything from the severance to the job lineup was very quiet. I'm sure it was a lot to digest all at once. I'm sure he was still at the "you are no longer with the company" part of the meeting. After a few minutes went by, Sean acknowledged that he was grateful for the severance and offer of a new career but that he would have to sit on it for a while.

About three months went by, and Sean contacted me to tell me that he had decided he didn't want to go into sales. He had another proposition that was far more appealing. A general contractor in the Tomball area north of Houston owned a Mexican restaurant called Tejas Grill and, after ten years in business, wanted to sell. Sean wanted my thoughts on the deal, and everything he mentioned sounded like a unique opportunity for him to get into the Tex-Mex business. The deal included not only the goodwill but also the real estate. Once Sean and the owner of Tejas Grill agreed on a purchase price, the owner got cold feet and wanted to back out because he wasn't sure if Sean had enough experience in operations to be successful long-term.

That was a valid concern since Sean's dealings with operations at Gringo's were minimal, if any. Sean asked me to speak with the owner, which I did, and I assured him that we would be a resource for Sean with anything he needed to be successful. They finally inked the deal, and today, Sean is the happiest I've ever seen him. And Tejas Grill is doing extremely well. Sean has been able to increase sales while at the same time improving margins simply by building on his relationships with vendors during his time at Gringo's.

I'm sharing this story because I believe the process of terminating an employee is as important, if not more so, than when you hire them. Here is why. I don't believe in burning bridges when it comes to employee-employer relationships that may have started great but maybe didn't end so well. What's important is that both parties end their relationship the same way it started, with a handshake. Our second core value—fostering honesty and respect among our team members—is how Gringo's has been able to maintain a reputation for being a great place to work.

What has made Gringo's very special over the years are our people—our employees. We call them our team members. Many of them joined me as young twenty-year-olds, while others were mere teenagers. Many of them are now in their early forties and have given me and Gringo's some of their best years in terms of earning potential.

I'm grateful that they have done this, and I never want to forget that single fact. Just like a guest has many choices when dining out, and they chose us for Tex-Mex, so does the individual when choosing a company to work for. I'm proud to say that Sean and I talk to each other all the time about the business and how a potentially negative decision to terminate someone has instead turned into a long-lasting friendship.

So how do you surround yourself with people who make you better? Find the ones who are doing what you want to do at an excellent level and glean all you can from them. And in return, you respect and appreciate what each individual brings to the table. You lead by example of what you aspire to be so that those around you can have a blueprint for what you want to create. When you create an atmosphere of high quality, you will attract those with the same mindset. They will come through word of mouth, trade associations, chambers of commerce, vendors, and everyone you come in contact with. Remember, this takes time. It's about having the patience required to develop long-term relationships that will help you get closer to your goals.

To-Go Items ~~~~~~~~~~~~~~~~~~~~~~~~~~~~~~~~~~~

1. If you have a dream, you need a team.

2. Every business owner must have enough self-awareness to understand what they are good at—and what they are not.

3. The process of terminating an employee is as important, if not more so, than hiring them.

CHAPTER 6

Don't Let Fear of Failure Paralyze You

~~~~~~

Most great people have attained their greatest success just one step beyond their greatest failure.

—NAPOLEON HILL, *Think and Grow Rich*

The defining moment in my life occurred at exactly 11:00 a.m. on January 11, 1993. That day, I had no choice but to face my fears head on. Deep inside of me, I was scared and very concerned about what the future held for me. After all, who in their right mind would think they could actually turn around a property where four other restaurants had previously failed and make it work this time?

The only tools I had to work with were all the good and bad

lessons I had experienced up to that point in my life. I had no choice but to go forward and not allow the real possibility of failing to stop me once again. That day, I was introduced to my other self. Prior to the day Gringo's opened for business, every one of my past failures had forced me to see business in a completely different light. They made me realize that if I were ever going to be successful in business, then my approach would have to be different, which meant making money was no longer my primary focus. Instead, I would focus all my energy on producing a high-quality, consistent product and price it lower than or equal to the competition.

In *Think and Grow Rich*, Napoleon Hill makes this statement:

> "Success requires no apologies, failure permits no alibis." . . . [E]very failure brings with it the seed of an equivalent success. Henry Ford, poor and uneducated, dreamed of a horseless carriage. He went to work with the tools he possessed, without waiting for an opportunity to favor him. . . .
>
> Practical dreamers do not quit! . . . [A]ll who succeed in life usually get off to a bad start, and pass through many heartbreaking struggles before they "arrive." The turning point in the lives of those who succeed usually comes at the moment of some crisis through which they are introduced to their "other selves."[18]

---

18 Napoleon Hill, *Think and Grow Rich*, deluxe ed. (New York: Penguin, 2008), 31, 33–34.

Many things worth having in life can sometimes only be reachable by going over to the other side of fear and facing it head-on. Most people who dream of going into business will overthink their plans. They do this because they believe that for them to be successful, they must have the perfect plan. In some ways, I can't blame them, but unfortunately, there is no such thing as the perfect plan. A person cannot think their way toward perfection; they must face their fear and act, and from that action, they will evolve by knowing that absolute perfection is unattainable.

BURN THE BOATS!

I remember reading about how a person will always exhibit a greater commitment to moving forward instead of hesitating and staying put if they would simply use the analogy of "burning the boats" to help them leap forward toward their goals and dreams of success. The analogy comes from a legendary tale about Spanish explorer Hernan Cortes.

In 1519, Cortes wanted to capture the treasure that the Aztecs were holding. To meet his goals, he landed several ships with five hundred soldiers and over one hundred sailors on the Yucatan shore. Despite the large contingent of men, he was still greatly outnumbered by the large Aztec empire on land.

Some of the men in Cortes's army began questioning their leader, fearing that this nearly impossible mission would only end in failure. A few of the doubting ringleaders plotted to return to their vessels and escape to nearby Cuba.

When Cortes learned of this plan to flee, he came up with a plan to guarantee his men would focus on their one united mission of capturing the treasure and making it impossible for the men to escape. Cortes commanded, "Burn our ships!" Naturally, the men at first resisted this seemingly insane directive, as they knew they weren't going to be able to return home. Cortes's response was, "Well then, if we want to return home, we are going to have to defeat the Aztecs and take their ships!"[19]

After this, the men had no choice but to face their fear and march forward.

His plan was simple—with their ships taken out of the picture, any possibility of failure was also removed. They would have to have 100 percent dedication to the cause in order to succeed and return home in their enemy's ships. And they did exactly that.

Like Cortes, there was no turning back for me once I pulled the string to the neon "open" sign. I had nothing else to fall back on if Gringo's ended up failing. I had no education or skill set. No one that I knew of expected Gringo's to succeed. The odds were against me. Opening up a restaurant in a building where four other restaurants had already failed isn't the wisest thing to do for anyone, myself included.

---

19   Donald Smith, "Sometimes It's Best to Burn Your Ships," *ME&A*, September 7, 2022, https://www.meandahq.com/sometimes-its-best-to-burn-your-ships/.

LESSONS IN CONSISTENCY

Whenever someone contacts me and asks if I would consider meeting with them to discuss a business idea, I always say yes. Since I live in Houston and our corporate offices are located in La Porte, and because we have restaurants located throughout the Houston area, I always try to arrange our meeting at a location that is convenient for whomever I'm meeting with. My desire to accommodate comes from an experience I had earlier in my career.

In 1986, I helped launch El Matador Tortilla Company because I had decided that I was no longer going to remain in the restaurant business. During that time, the only restaurants that used tortilla products were other Mexican restaurants. Unfortunately, I had a lot of difficulty selling tortilla products to them because of guilt by association. Meaning most of the Mexican restaurants I tried selling tortillas to would not buy from me simply because of our family-owned El Toro Mexican Restaurants. I don't blame them necessarily—that's just the way it was, and I accepted it.

That dilemma didn't stop me from trying. Fortunately, one particular individual didn't mind the fact that my family's restaurants were also some of his competitors, and that person was Larry Forehand with Casa Olé. I remember calling on Larry once from my driveway while sitting in my Mazda B2000 pickup truck, requesting an appointment so I could show him my product line. I was so nervous talking to Larry that I didn't have enough oxygen to get the words out of my mouth! I viewed Larry as a celebrity of sorts because he was such a giant in the restaurant industry. I couldn't believe he was willing to speak with me, much less allow me to show him our tortilla product line.

Larry started off in the restaurant industry at age fourteen, working as a busboy for Monterrey House in Houston. He became a manager at age eighteen before being drafted during the Vietnam War. After completing his military service, Larry went back to work for Monterrey House, and in 1973, at age twenty-nine, he opened his first Casa Olé on Southmore Street in Pasadena, Texas. It became one of the busiest Mexican restaurants around. He and his partner Mike Domec grew the company to over fifty-five locations throughout Texas and Louisiana.

I wanted to sell our six-inch flour tortillas to Casa Olé for serving alongside their fajita dinners. The equipment we were using to manufacture this particular item wasn't new; we had purchased it from another tortilla company in Austin because they were setting up a new state-of-the-art flour tortilla line. Although this machine wasn't the best, it did allow us to press up to nine six-inch tortillas per cycle, ten cycles a minute.

This was considered a decent production rate, but that wasn't the issue. The problem was the machine would not press all the tortillas evenly; they came out in different sizes and thicknesses. The oven we used to bake the tortillas was also pre-owned and caused the tortillas to bake unevenly. To make sure the samples I dropped off to Larry were perfect, I handpicked them. I know I shouldn't have tried to hide the quality issues, and it was just a matter of time before that came back to bite me.

After about six months of selling our flour tortillas to Casa

Olé, they dropped our account because of—big surprise—product inconsistency. It was tough losing the account. However, to again quote Napoleon Hill, "Every failure brings with it the seed of an equivalent success."[20] In the long run, it was a very valuable lesson because I learned the importance of consistency.

Today, a primary focus at Gringo's and Jimmy Changas is to make sure that no matter what we serve, it must be consistent. We are continually evaluating systems and procedures to ensure that no matter what we prepare, it will be consistent. For example, one of those consistency systems includes using custom, prepackaged spice bags, an idea I "borrowed" from Casa Olé. This procedure ensures that a batch of taco meat at Gringo's in Pearland will taste exactly the same as the taco meat at the Gringo's in College Station.

Larry not only was a pioneer in the Mexican food industry but also opened the door to a young twenty-six-year-old entrepreneur and gave him a chance to succeed. At the time, it was what I needed to push forward with the business. Because of what Larry did for me so many years ago, I have met and will continue to meet with the next generation of business entrepreneurs.

When I resigned from El Matador in 1992 to open up Gringo's a few months later, I used El Matador as our tortilla supplier from the very first day of business, not just because it is the company I helped start up during the '80s (and which my family still

---

20 Napoleon Hill, *Become Your Best* (Mumbai: Jaico, 2015), 187.

operates), but also because I understood the difficulty in growing that kind of business.

During our first year in business at Gringo's, we purchased approximately $11,000 worth of tortilla products. In 2022, we purchased almost $4 million worth of products from them. El Matador has been able to modernize its production by investing in state-of-the-art equipment, which has allowed it to increase consistency and productivity and expand its customer base throughout Texas and beyond. I'm extremely proud to know that Gringo's and Jimmy Changas have played a major role in its growth and success.

A NO-GEAUX

In October 2006, we opened up a seafood restaurant concept called Gringaux's Seafood Kitchen next door to our Gringo's in Stafford. The restaurant never generated the sales we were hoping for, so we decided to close it just over a year later. A friend of mine, who is also in the restaurant business, gave me some "words of wisdom" soon after closing Gringaux's Seafood Kitchen.

He said, "Russell, the restaurant business is like baseball. As long as you're batting a high average, you'll do okay." I must admit, at the time, those were the best words I could've heard at that very moment. Failing did not feel good; nor did it taste good. But in some ways, I'm glad I experienced it. I was able to take away some invaluable lessons that have helped me continue to grow and prosper.

This failure did hit differently because, up to this point, we had already opened seven successful Gringo's locations. I believe that this one failure alone helped our entire leadership team see Gringo's in a completely different light. That no matter who we hire to design, build, or manage our restaurants, it does not guarantee success. It will forever be known as my 3.2-million-dollar seafood platter!

APPEARANCES CAN BE DISTRACTING

One thing that can paralyze you with fear is worrying about how others see you—it's a fear of pursuing your dreams because you're more afraid of what others will think of you should you end up failing.

You don't have to look much further than the social media site Instagram to see a world built on nothing but smoke and mirrors. It's a place where a person would much rather appear a certain way even though they may not be anywhere near it. Instagram, Facebook, and X (formerly known as Twitter) all serve a purpose. They're tools that, if used properly, can be a good thing for connecting with others.

But it seems many people want to be perceived by others as being successful at something before they really are. To them, the only thing that does matter is how they appear to everyone else. That's a huge mistake, in my opinion, because it can cause a person to lose focus on what they should be doing to achieve a better life. When a person is more concerned about how they appear to others than the reality of where they're at in life, it can turn into a slippery slope they sometimes never recover from. This image game can keep you from achieving your goals. Some people will remain stagnant in pursuing their dreams because they are more worried about how other people see them than the dream itself.

I can remember working in the kitchen at El Toro as a teenager. Whenever one of the line cooks would quit to work for a construction company, inevitably, they'd always return to the restaurant on a Friday evening to show their former coworkers their check stubs and brag about how much more they were earning now. Being proud of what you earn is one thing, but it is rude and condescending to show someone else your pay stub, especially when you know they are earning less than you. Showing off is human nature, but left unchecked, it can also distract you from your full potential by focusing you on the wrong things. Appearance is important, but what's more important are your words followed by your actions. Without those, a person will only go so far with their career.

FACING MY GREATEST FEAR

In 2015, I experienced a medical emergency that put all my fears—including the fear of failure—into perspective.

That year, I started to experience what I thought were high levels of anxiety when Monica and I would return home after a nice dinner and drinks at a favorite restaurant. The feeling would be located between my lower chest and stomach area. The best way I can describe it is that it felt like serious indigestion accompanied by anxiety and restlessness.

At first, this feeling would last for only a few minutes, but it got progressively worse. This went on for a couple of years. In June 2017, after a longer attack, I finally went to see my primary physician. He immediately ordered an ultrasound, and the results showed that I had a large number of gallstones. He told me to avoid alcohol—usually not a problem, except I was traveling soon to see some favorite bands, particularly U2, in concert. I powered through the no-alcohol sacrifice, though.

Fast-forward to August 16, 2017. I was scheduled to have lunch with my franchise partner, Joel Perkins, in the Woodlands at the recently opened Goode Company BBQ. I wanted to check out the restaurant because it was one of the prototypes of their newest concept, a barbecue and Tex-Mex brand under one roof, called Goode Company Kitchen and Cantina. I ordered my usual sliced brisket and jalapeño sausage with coleslaw and beans, sauce on the side. After I finished, I began to experience a bit of nausea. I didn't think much about it, but the feeling stayed with me most of the day. Later that afternoon, I was supposed to meet Monica's family, who were visiting from California, at the Top Golf located in Webster. I was the first one to arrive at around five o'clock. Since I was still feeling queasy, I decided to order sparkling water to see if that would help settle the nausea. It didn't.

It only seemed to get worse, and I couldn't keep from vomiting. At this point, I knew something was seriously wrong. I told Monica that I needed to go home, about thirty miles away. As I neared home, traffic slowed to a crawl, and that's when the pain of all pains kicked in.

I didn't know it at the time, but I was experiencing a severe pancreatitis attack, which is the sudden inflammation of the pancreas. Once I got home, I realized I had to call 911. I hit all three numbers on the landline phone before realizing the phone wasn't plugged in. Shaking my head, I got the phone fixed and finally dialed. The West University EMS arrived in less than five minutes.

When the ambulance pulled up to the house, I didn't wait for them to knock on the door; I met them in the street. I called Monica from the ambulance on the way to Methodist Hospital and gave her the news.

When we arrived at the emergency room and they rolled me into the waiting area, I couldn't help but notice all the commotion going on around me. At the same time, it felt like I was dying. It was such a surreal moment, mainly because I still didn't know exactly what was going on with me. I texted my good friend Michael Berry to see if he knew a doctor at Methodist that he could recommend.

Fortunately, he did—Dr. Prasanth R. Boyareddigari—who ordered my blood work not long after I arrived at the ER. After what felt like hours, mainly because of the sheer pain I was in, they finally rolled me away for an ultrasound and then to be admitted. Luckily for me, Michael showed up just when they were about to finalize my hospital room and told them to "put Russell in Fondren 12, and that's an order." I had never before heard of Fondren 12, but apparently Michael had. It was a private suite with a couch and its own bathroom. It was in that room that my fear turned into peace. I realized that fear would not help me, and I trusted the destiny God had for me.

I had two great doctors tending to me, Dr. Daniel Bonville and Dr. Sandeep Lahoti. The doctors knew exactly what was going on after seeing my blood test and ultrasound results. I was told I had a stuck gallstone blocking my common bile duct, causing bile to back up in my gallbladder and pancreas, leading to an acute pancreatitis attack.

Dr. Lahoti performed an endoscopic procedure the very next day to see if he could unblock the tiny gallstone causing me so much pain. No luck. I was put on an IV and was restricted from taking any food or liquid, including water, during my entire stay in the hospital. This was done so my body could turn off my organs from processing any digestion. The only positive benefit to not eating or drinking anything during my eight-day hospital stay was that I lost fifteen pounds.

I gave my doctors the green light to go ahead and perform the laparoscopic procedure to remove my gallbladder. The doctor would be making four small incisions around my stomach and inserting narrow tubes to guide the long, thin instruments used to manipulate, sew, and cut the tissue. There was no way I was going to experience that specific pain ever again, and if removing my gallbladder was the only way to accomplish that, then good-bye gallbladder.

Heading into surgery was a strange and surreal experience. I remember the nurses being so nice to me as I was rolled into the staging area to be prepped for the procedure. That operating room was so dang cold; I remember them putting a couple of warm blankets over me. They felt so good. The anesthesiologist began his procedure by placing the mask on my face, and I don't remember much else after that until I woke up in my hospital room.

My surgery to remove my gallbladder went very well, but it's a strange feeling coming out of that sleep after surgery; it's like rebooting your mind. The strangest thing was what I experienced right after surgery once I was awake. I described to Monica what I saw on the ceiling of my hospital room—pyramids and other Egyptian-like artifacts set in the desert moving like a motion picture—all while still fully aware of the reality of where I was. I was definitely tripping on whatever narcotic they gave me during surgery.

Obviously, I never want to experience that pain again, and I am certainly not eager to die or leave my family behind. But after going through all of that, I am no longer afraid, and I feel like I have had more than an extra portion of my life. When it is my time, I want to leave a legacy behind that will serve others for many years to come.

To-Go Items

1. You cannot think your way to perfection. You must face your fears and act.

2. Find the lesson in each failure and use it to build success.

3. Don't be paralyzed with fear from worrying about how others see you. The image game can keep you from achieving your goals.

CHAPTER 7

Develop a Sense of Urgency

~~~~~~

Without a sense of urgency, desire loses its value.

—ATTRIBUTED TO JIM ROHN

When I franchised a Gringo's to Joel Perkins for the first time in 2000, we ran into a problem during the remodel. Since the remodel included mostly painting and minor carpentry work, we decided not to pull a building permit from the city of Houston. One area we decided to improve was the kitchen drains. This kitchen had standard four-inch round drains, but we preferred the four-foot trench drains in our other kitchens because they made it easier for our staff to wash down the floors at closing time.

While we were in the process of installing the trench drains, we were visited early one morning by a city of Houston building inspector. He saw that we did not have a permit to install the floor drains, so he immediately issued us a "red tag," meaning we were to stop all work until we submitted a stamped set of drawings by a licensed plumbing engineer to receive a permit.

I knew a couple who might be able to help us—Houston architect Davis Wilson and his wife, Diane, who ran a permitting service inside his office. A longtime designer of restaurants in the Houston area, Davis had helped me build the second Gringo's from the ground up, and I had relied on his real estate expertise as well. Now, I called on Davis to help with the permitting situation. Knowing how long the permitting process could take, I was hopeful that Davis and Diane could help us receive a permit in about two to three weeks. When I spoke to Davis over the phone, he told me to sketch out the kitchen floor plan on a piece of paper, show exactly where all of the drains would be installed, and fax it over to him. I did that the same morning we were inspected.

Because of the relationships Diane had built over the years with Houston's permitting department, we were issued a permit to continue installing the trench drains that same afternoon. This was an absolute miracle because that kind of turnaround—less than eight hours after we were issued a red tag—in a permitting department simply does not happen every day. Time is money in business, and Davis and Diane helped us save a lot of both. Their sense of urgency got me out of that bind, as well as plenty of others over the years.

When Davis closed down his office several years later, he called to see if I was interested in purchasing a vintage nickel slot machine that he used to have on display in his reception area. He told me the slot machine was worth $5,000. I could have haggled with him for a lower price, but instead, I told Davis to have someone deliver it to my office, and there would be a check waiting for the delivery driver at the receptionist's desk. Today, that slot machine sits in my office as a reminder of how important relationships are to a businessperson's success and how Davis is responsible for a part of mine.

I responded to Davis's request for me to purchase his slot machine with the exact same sense of urgency he exhibited on my behalf years prior.

PEOPLE OVER PAPER

How many times have you visited a business, such as a tire shop, to purchase a new set of tires for your car, and you stood at the counter waiting for someone to acknowledge your presence? Sometimes, it takes so long that you begin to feel like you're invisible.

This happens when a person prioritizes their needs over the needs of others. Instead, you should prioritize the needs of others over your own—and with a sense of urgency. When you do this, you give this person something they will compare other businesses to, especially the competition. The number one goal of every business should be to be better today than they were yesterday. Even a 1 percent improvement daily adds up over time. Every business's motto should be *people over paper*. Whatever an employee is busy doing at a particular moment will never be more important than the needs of a waiting customer unless they're busy tending to another customer. But even a simple acknowledgment, saying "I'll be right with you," goes a long way in making a customer not feel invisible.

A sense of urgency also comes into play when dealing with any customer issues, whether in person or online. For a problem with a takeout order, for example, a guest will usually send me an email almost immediately after realizing that something is wrong with their order. Because I understand how frustrated they are at that specific moment, and because it's so fresh on their mind, I don't want to add to their aggravation by making them wait for a response from our company. Whenever I receive an email in regard to a customer complaint with their to-go order, I stop what I'm doing and respond almost immediately.

Even if I'm on vacation or right in the middle of doing something that is important to me, I will immediately reply to their email with a message such as the following one.

Dear [Name],

First and foremost, I sincerely apologize for making a mistake with your to-go order. I promise that we will make it up to you. Please provide me with a contact number and a time when you can be reached, and I'll have one of our team members get back to you within forty-eight hours.

And last, thank you for choosing us when dining out for Tex-Mex. It means everything to me and our entire team.

This response is short and sweet, but it also gives our guests peace of mind, knowing that they will be taken care of. More importantly, it shows we care—because we do. Given the sheer amount of to-go volume we generate and the large number of team members required to fulfill a single order, we will make mistakes from time to time. With each guest's feedback telling us we left something out of their order, the order was entered wrong, or whatever the situation may be, we like to take that feedback and analyze it to improve our systems so we don't repeat it.

It's not what happens day to day in business that causes you to succeed or fail but rather how you respond to what happens—and what kind of urgency you bring to that response. A business must operate with a high level of appreciation whenever a customer walks into their place of business because a customer can easily sense whether or not a business truly appreciates their patronage. Your competition only has to show the consumer that they care more about them than you do, and guess who wins them over?

You would think that after thirty years of business, we would be at a place that completely eliminates mistakes. I wish that were possible, but unfortunately, it's not. There are just too many working parts. A guest complaint is simply an *opportunity* to resell the customer again, and in many cases, how you handle the situation can make them loyal customers for life. A customer complaint that's quickly resolved can bond the customer and business closer, and that person will become an ambassador for the brand.

THE WRONG RESPONSE

While having a sense of urgency when responding to your customers is vital, there's also a right and a wrong way to respond. The previous example was the right way. Now, let's look at the wrong way.

I was having breakfast recently with a good friend of mine when he introduced me to one of his longtime business acquaintances. After learning that I was in the restaurant business, we started discussing some of the challenges that come along with it, specifically dealing with guests' complaints. He shared a story with me about how he and a friend got very sick after eating at one of Houston's premier fine-dining restaurants one Friday evening. He called the restaurant back the next morning to let them know, and the hostess who answered the phone said a manager would call him right back.

A little more than forty-eight hours went by before the restaurant's general manager finally called to learn more about the situation. After explaining to the manager that they believed it was the gumbo that got both of them sick, the manager's only response was, "We use only the finest ingredients." That was it. No apology. No empathy. No effort to make things right. And by waiting two days to call back, the manager had no sense of urgency in the response either.

Not surprisingly, this person went on to tell me that he's never been back to this restaurant. All because of the wrong response.

Look, it may or may not have been the gumbo that got them sick. That's not what's important to this story. What is important is that the manager should have first apologized and expressed a genuine concern for their well-being. Sometimes, that is all a guest wants to hear. A well-trained general manager could follow up by offering to refund their money or offer something complimentary on their next visit. The most important thing is to find out what will make them happy. The sooner a GM can respond to a guest after learning that they did not enjoy their food or service, the sooner they can offer some sort of remedy that is satisfactory and fair to the customer.

If a customer returns to a business after a negative experience and all the business did to make them happy was refund their money, then the business wins because they didn't end up losing a customer. Why lose a longtime or potential new customer just because they may get the impression that a business doesn't care enough to exhibit some degree of empathy or a sense of urgency?

Statistics show that most customers don't quit a company because of bad service; they quit because of indifference. No sense of urgency. No demonstration of care. It costs much more money to gain a new customer than to keep an existing one by simply making sure they are satisfied after each visit.

Exhibiting empathy and a sense of urgency requires very

little effort. But it *does* take your time—something a customer will appreciate and that shows the business actually values their patronage.

A CULTURE OF URGENCY AND EMPATHY

John Calvin Maxwell, an American author, speaker, and pastor, teaches that everything rises and falls on leadership. That's especially true when it comes to establishing the type of culture you want to have in your business, and that applies not only to your customers but also to your staff. Exhibiting empathy and a sense of urgency is part of the culture at Gringo's. As part of that, I have an open-door policy with our team members, meaning any team member at any time can send an email directly to me should they ever feel that they have hit a brick wall with management regarding some matter or concern with their employment. I never want our company to make a team member feel like we're too busy to hear what they have to say. I cannot expect any team member to practice a sense of urgency with our guests unless I am willing to apply it with them as well. Whenever a company combines this important principle with their employees, along with a genuine concern for them and their well-being, the customer ultimately wins. And if the customer is satisfied and pleased, they'll return for more of what that business sells, and when this happens, everyone associated with the business also wins.

I like to remind my management teams that no matter what

kinds of challenges they face each day, our competitors will face similar ones. The only difference between them and us will be how we handle each situation with a high sense of urgency and empathy.

After our team members, every single guest we serve is extremely important to me (thus, our first core value—developing guest relations one meal at a time). Our guests are the only reason we are able to pay our bills. I want to show them how important they are to our success by always seeing our restaurant through their eyes. If I can get our entire team to feel the same way, then there's really no stopping us from continuing to grow and improve at every level of our operation.

On a more practical note, punctuality in the restaurant business is extremely important, so a sense of urgency must be inherent. As noted previously, for us to meet and exceed what our guests expect from us, everything my team members do revolves around time. The time it takes to greet them at the front, seat them, take their drink order, take their food order, prepare and deliver an order—you get the picture. So, as the team leader, I set the example of being punctual with everything I do. When I do so, my team members will follow suit, resulting in a timelier operation. We also live in a time when the consumer's patience is extremely short because almost any product or service that used to take days to receive now only takes seconds to order and, in some cases, minutes to get. Technology is responsible for most of this, along with a very conditioned consumer. The race for most businesses is to get ahead of the competition by utilizing the latest technology to streamline every area of their business. Because of that, applying a sense of urgency is probably more relevant today than ever before because of technology.

When I worked at El Toro Restaurant during the late '80s, we offered home delivery, but this was way before technology changed everything and gave us Uber Eats, Grubhub, and DoorDash. Back then, placing a to-go order would look something like this: One of the three telephone landlines would ring, and the cashier would answer it. The customer on the other line would say that they would like to place an order for delivery. They would then ask the cashier to describe a couple of the items on the menu along with the prices. Then, after the customer finally told the cashier what they wanted to order, the cashier would ask for their address and how they were going to pay for it—cash, check, or credit card. If it were cash, the cashier would ask what denomination they were going to use so that we could send the correct change to the delivery driver. The cashier would then walk the ticket over to the kitchen to be prepared.

After it was ready for delivery, one of the delivery drivers employed by the restaurant would grab their KeyMap (a map that showed all the streets in a particular zip code or the Google Maps of that era) to try and find where they'd be making the delivery. After dropping off the order, the delivery driver would then return to the restaurant, give the sales proceeds to the cashier, and go back to the storeroom and wait there until there was another order to deliver. This process was so inefficient and time-consuming that El Toro suspended the free delivery service after only a few years.

Today, it only requires a few clicks, and you can have just about anything you're craving delivered directly to you from one of your favorite restaurants. You don't even need to interact with the delivery driver. I once ordered a salad from Chick-fil-A, and from the time I entered my order on my iPhone to the time it was delivered to me at the office was only fifteen minutes. That is very fast by any measure.

Developing a sense of urgency in everything you do will automatically make you stand out and be appreciated.

BEING THERE FOR OTHERS

The most important aspect of practicing a sense of urgency is not doing something for someone in an urgent manner simply because you expect something from them in return. Instead, you do it because if you were to ever find yourself in a situation where you needed help, someone might just be there for you.

During a trip to Loreto, Mexico, to play golf with Jonathan Kim, my son Steve, and my brother Roland (president of El Toro Restaurants), I received a private message from Cynthia, daughter of one of our team members, Veronica. Veronica had recently passed away from complications associated with COVID-19. She had given Gringo's over twenty years of service.

Cynthia contacted me from the funeral home where she was

making burial arrangements for her mother. We had already promised Cynthia that as a gesture of our appreciation for the years her mother gave to Gringo's, we would take care of the funeral expenses. She had contacted me to give me the total amount due and to let me know it needed to be paid that day. I immediately stopped hitting practice balls and contacted my chief marketing officer, Heather McKeon, to handle the situation. Since I was in Mexico, the reception with my cell phone wasn't very strong, and I kept losing contact with Heather each time I called her. I kept trying until I was finally able to get ahold of her and explain Cynthia's dilemma. Heather knew exactly what to do and contacted the funeral home immediately.

In situations like this, especially when it involves a team member who's been with the company for so many years, I just put myself in their shoes and ask, "How would I want this handled if I was the one asking for help during these most trying of times?"

When a person loses a loved one, everything in your world is in a whirlwind at that moment. And there's nothing worse than having to wait for someone when you need them the most simply because they're too busy for you. Honestly, I wouldn't have been able to live with myself if I hadn't handled the situation immediately, knowing that Veronica gave Gringo's her best years, which is the entire reason I was able to stand where I was in the first place.

I firmly believe that every single act of kindness and compassion you exhibit toward others, especially when you exhibit a sense of urgency, you are also doing to and for yourself.

I don't usually like to go around wearing my faith on my sleeve, but Cynthia and Veronica's story reminds me of a powerful passage in Matthew 25:31–46 about the Final Judgment:

> When the Son of Man comes in his glory, and all the angels with him, then he will sit on his glorious throne. Before him will be gathered all the nations, and he will separate people one from another as a shepherd separates the sheep from the goats. And he will place the sheep on his right, but the goats on the left. Then the King will say to those on his right, "Come, you who are blessed by my Father, inherit the kingdom prepared for you from the foundation of the world. For I was hungry and you gave me food, I was thirsty and you gave me drink, I was a stranger and you welcomed me, I was naked and you clothed me, I was sick and you visited me, I was in prison and you came to me." Then the righteous will answer him, saying, "Lord, when did we see you hungry and feed you, or thirsty and give you drink? And when did we see you a stranger and welcome you, or naked and clothe you? And when did we see you sick or in prison and visit you?" And the King will

answer them, "Truly, I say to you, as you did it to one of the least of these my brothers, you did it to me."

Then he will say to those on his left, "Depart from me, you cursed, into the eternal fire prepared for the devil and his angels. For I was hungry and you gave me no food, I was thirsty and you gave me no drink, I was a stranger and you did not welcome me, naked and you did not clothe me, sick and in prison and you did not visit me." Then they also will answer, saying, "Lord, when did we see you hungry or thirsty or a stranger or naked or sick or in prison, and did not minister to you?" Then he will answer them, saying, "Truly, I say to you, as you did not do it to one of the least of these, you did not do it to me." And these will go away into eternal punishment, but the righteous into eternal life.[21]

I don't know about you, but I certainly want to be on the right side when that time comes!

---

21 Matt. 25:31–46 (English Standard Version).

To-Go Items

1. Every business's motto should be people over paper.

2. It's not what happens day to day in a business that causes you to succeed or fail but how you respond to what happens and the urgency in that response.

3. A customer complaint that's quickly resolved can bond the customer and business.

4. Exhibiting empathy and a sense of urgency requires little but your time—something customers will appreciate.

5. Apply a sense of urgency when dealing with your employees. Never let them feel you are too busy to hear what they have to say.

CHAPTER 8

Take Responsibility for Your Actions

A good leader takes a little more than his share of the blame, a little less than his share of the credit.

—ATTRIBUTED TO ARNOLD H. GLASOW

*D*o as I say, not as I do. If put into practice, these are probably the most detrimental words to a restaurant operator. A business will eventually dissipate over time if a manager says one thing yet does another. Leading by example is the strongest management style a manager can exhibit for their staff.

I consider all our team members an extension of myself. I never expect an employee of Gringo's to do anything that I wouldn't be willing to do myself. My hope is that their future actions will reflect what I would do in any given situation. I trust them to take responsibility for their actions and that they will always use good judgment.

One of the most important reasons why a person must learn the habit of taking responsibility for their actions is because it opens an opportunity for them to gain a deeper understanding of their true self. And this can eventually lead to greater rewards over a lifetime. This habit of personal responsibility is difficult because it forces a person to look inward and find the reason why they are in a certain situation. But the most beautiful aspect of this habit is it also allows a person to find their solution.

One of the things I really appreciated about working for my father at a very young age was that no matter how many times I made a mistake, he never once criticized me for doing so. Because of this, I was never intimidated about trying something new in the restaurants, whether it was creating a new dish, remodeling a dining room, trying different ingredients, or coming up with a marketing promotion that may not have done so well. All of these things that I was allowed to do and sometimes failed at helped me at a young age take responsibility for my own actions. I have worked to establish a culture of personal responsibility at Gringo's, starting with myself. Beyond taking responsibility for your mistakes, this habit lends itself to handling tasks or situations that may not fall under your exact job description but still need to be done. And no employee should be considered above doing them—not even management.

Case in point: Several years ago, at our Pearland location, I went into the men's room and noticed a strong odor coming from the toilet stall. As I stood there, the stall door opened, and out came a small child, approximately five years old. He proceeded to wash his hands but had to jump up and rest on his stomach to reach the faucet water. I was glad to see him washing his hands. As he left the restroom, I peeked inside the stall to see what was causing this less-than-desirable odor. Sure enough, the child had not been able to reach the water part of the toilet and made a mess on the ceramic part of the toilet. I thought a flush or two would do the trick—but it didn't.

At that moment, I considered finding a busser and informing him that the restrooms needed their hourly check-up. Instead, I decided to take responsibility and clean up the situation myself.

I tell this story not to say that management should be assigned to restroom duty but that they should be willing to take care of any situation, no matter how unpleasant it may appear. We all lead by example. Period. Our actions will always speak louder than our words. So, next time one of our managers sees trash on the floor, I hope they will pick it up. If they see a guest needing a tea refill, I hope they won't wait for someone else to do it.

These simple actions will train your staff in ways that a classroom setting never can and never will. And last but not least, if you are heading to the bathroom and you notice a small child going ahead of you, you may want to wait awhile!

WHEN UNFORTUNATE THINGS HAPPEN

Just because something bad happens to you in life doesn't automatically mean someone else is at fault. Unfortunately, some in our society have been conditioned to believe that if something bad happens to them, then there has to be someone else responsible.

Shortly after we opened the Gringo's in La Porte, our liquor distributor was making a delivery, and the driver parked his truck in front of the restaurant to unload the order. He loaded the dolly with five cases of tequila and started to bring them into the building. Rather than rolling the dolly up the ramp in the front of the restaurant or the ramp connected to the kitchen dock located behind the restaurant, the delivery driver tried to pull the dolly up over the curb and save himself a few extra steps. As he was trying to hoist the heavy dolly, the weight of the five cases of tequila, combined with the fact that he was wearing tennis shoes and the sidewalk was damp from the morning dew, caused him to lose his footing. He ended up falling and breaking his leg.

Sure enough, the delivery driver hired an attorney and filed a lawsuit against us, seeking unspecified damages. We chose to fight the lawsuit rather than settle it. We didn't believe we did anything wrong to cause his injury and that it was the fault of the driver for not using the two ramps that were available to him. Well, fortunately for us, the jury saw it the same way as we did, and the driver was awarded nothing.

Sometimes, unfortunate things just happen to people. Going through life always believing others are responsible for your circumstances will never get you anywhere. I would've been the first person to admit fault if, in fact, we were responsible.

LEARN FROM YOUR MISTAKES

The best defense for any business is to have a great offense. We have discovered at Gringo's that we cannot have too many security cameras installed throughout our restaurants. Just about every square inch of our newer buildings has cameras installed so we can record the numerous incidents that take place. We are constantly evaluating our properties to make sure there are no blind spots.

We trust our employees, but the cameras are there for everyone's benefit. If an incident occurs on our premises where a guest is injured, and the video shows that we are responsible, we have no issue with being held responsible and will gladly cover any costs incurred by the guest. But at the same time, we should not be held liable if a person walks into our establishment with the sole intention of staging a fake injury or if a guest plants a foreign object in their food at the end of a meal so that they can get it free. This has happened on a few occasions over the last thirty years in business.

Plus, we have had some interesting incidents take place in our restaurants where, if a camera had not been there to catch it, we would never have believed it. A few years back, one of our kitchen team members was wiping down the exhaust hood after the restaurant had closed. This team member decided that, rather than use the ladder for the job, he would stand directly on top of the cooking equipment underneath the exhaust hood to complete the work. As he was walking across each piece of equipment under the hood, he lost his footing near the large deep fryer and fell in feet first. The oil hadn't cooled down and was still extremely hot. While he jumped out quickly, he did end up receiving some serious burns and had to get a small skin graft performed on both feet. All things considered, he is doing okay today.

In this particular situation, the company hadn't done anything negligent to cause this accident. The employee acknowledged his negligent conduct, but as the employer, we are still responsible for the well-being of our team members no matter who is negligent, so we ended up covering 100 percent of his medical bills and lost wages. And we're perfectly fine with that. This team member did return to work once he made a full recovery, but if there's one thing I'm confident of, it's that he will never do that again.

HANDLING CONFLICTS

Conflicts throughout one's lifetime are going to happen; there's almost no way of avoiding them. Whenever one does arise, your objective should be to get through it without damaging your relationship or your reputation (see Chapter 3). However, you also must be willing to take responsibility for your actions, no matter the situation.

This is important because it requires you to realize that, more often than not, you play a part in every situation or experience and, therefore, have some degree of responsibility over the out-comes or consequences.

A dispute shouldn't always be all about winning or losing; it's more about being able to see into the future and what the outcome might look like down the road. This requires a person to stand back and simply pause for a moment so as not to make an unnecessary mistake in judgment.

With any dispute, never allow your emotions to get ahead of the facts. Facts are the most important part of anything. In words attributed to Pythagoras, "No man is free who cannot control himself."

I learned this lesson the hard way when I let my emotions get the better of me in an unthought-out response to an employee whose work wasn't satisfactory. In the early 2000s, Gringo's hired a full-time person to maintain three of our properties. For this story, I'll refer to him as "Gordon."

Gordon wasn't performing up to expectations, but we continued to work with him, hoping he would improve. He never did. Apparently, he must have gotten a vibe from us that we weren't satisfied with the job he was doing. While I was at my office one Saturday morning, he popped in and asked me point blank if I was happy with his work.

I responded, "No, Gordon, to be very honest with you, I am not."

He didn't say anything else and walked out of my office. I immediately realized that I had made a mistake in giving him that answer. I just didn't know what the result would be.

About two weeks later, Gringo's received a letter from an attorney stating that Gordon had sustained an on-the-job injury at one of his assigned locations and the lawyer would be representing him.

We suspected that Gordon believed he would eventually be terminated, so instead of waiting for that moment, he chose to fake an injury while he was still employed by us. During the discovery period of the lawsuit, Gordon was examined by a doctor who wrote in his report that Gordon was inconsistent with the location and severity of his pain.

We chose to hire a private investigator to follow Gordon for two weeks. Sure enough, the investigator obtained video of Gordon performing physical acts that, according to the lawsuit, would have been impossible to do.

We later found out that Gordon had injured himself at his previous job, but not before we ended up settling the lawsuit during mediation.

When I look back on this particular situation and think about what I did wrong, here is what I will never do again involving an employee: If there is even the slightest possibility that I may end up needing to terminate someone, I will never say to their face that I am dissatisfied with their work unless I intend to terminate them at that very same moment.

Most of the time, whenever a mistake is made, or a conflict arises, a person's first reaction might be to blame others or make excuses. The sooner a person acknowledges there is a problem and that they may have played a role in it, the sooner it can be resolved. While conflicts between people will never be eliminated, minimizing damage should be the ultimate goal.

None of us can predict our future or the mistakes we will make, but each one of us can shape that future through the good habits we develop, the good choices we make, and the kinds of people we choose to have in our lives. If you spend a lot of time around people who are always constantly mad at the world, frustrated with their circumstances, or believe everyone is out to get them in one way or another, those feelings will influence you in a negative way. Soon, you'll start to believe that others are responsible for your actions and circumstances instead of you. Seek out and find positive messages to begin shaping your thoughts so that you can get closer to achieving your goals in life.

To-Go Items

1. Taking responsibility for your actions opens up the opportunity to gain a deeper understanding of your true self.

2. You play a part in every situation or experience and, therefore, have some degree of responsibility over the outcomes or consequences.

3. Never let emotions get ahead of the facts in a dispute.

4. While conflicts will never be eliminated, seek to minimize damage when dealing with one.

CHAPTER 9

Live Way below Your Means

If you live like no one else now, later,
you can live and *give* like no one else.

—**DAVE RAMSEY,** Twitter post

Your spending habits today will have a major impact on your future success. Being financially responsible is important. To live way below your means is to spend less than what you earn. That is much easier said than done, but it is something that must be done to maintain your health and financial well-being.

When my wife, Monica, and I first got married, there was a lot more love between us than there was money. As a matter of fact, our wedding was so low-budget that Monica's wedding dress was rented, and our guests were served on cheap paper plates at the reception. I sold my drum set for $800 to buy her wedding ring. The funny thing is that, at the time, we were both absolutely oblivious to it all.

We lived in a small garage apartment next door to my parents' house; my parents were our landlord. Fortunately for us, the rent was cheap, only a couple hundred dollars a month. Because I was only earning $300 a week, Monica would try to go days without spending even a penny. She would drive to the laundromat once a week to do our laundry. She would also, on occasion, go to a thrift store to buy her clothes. There aren't many young brides I know who'd be willing to do that, no matter how bad things got.

Even today, with our being financially well off, Monica still doesn't spend money like some people would if they were in her position. She lives well within her means.

That attitude is rooted in her upbringing. Monica grew up with a blue-collar working father who spoke very little English. She remembers how her stay-at-home mother would buy only generic brand groceries, and going out to eat was an occasional treat and a memorable one.

Money was always a factor in any decision in her household, but never in a negative way. It was simply managing what little money they had to maintain the household. No extras, no frills, and especially never buying anything to try and impress their neighbors.

A lot of people have gone broke over the years trying to look rich. The keeping-up-with-the-Joneses philosophy has hurt a lot of families financially. I completely understand that there are a lot of wants in life that border on actual needs. But it's important to understand the differences. The one number every person must know is how much money they have available to spend each month, and then know exactly where each dollar is being spent. In other words, it is important to have a budget.

One of the biggest misconceptions people have about wealthy people is that they're always spending money. If anything, wealthy people enjoy seeing their money grow rather than spending it on stuff that doesn't increase in value over time.

When it comes to accumulating wealth, there needs to be a balance between earning money and spending it.

WASTE NOT—WANT NOT!

One of my pet peeves in the restaurant business, not to mention in my everyday life, is wastefulness. Waste is money.

The habit of being wasteful can carry over into every area of a person's life. For example, although serving myself more food than I can eat at an all-you-can-eat buffet will not cost me any extra money, it's the mindset of not caring that ultimately will. Habits are habits, good or bad. Until a person changes their habits regarding waste, it will end up costing them money in the long run.

Growing up in a family of eight children, and despite my parents' ability to provide us with all the necessities in life, my mother taught me some valuable lessons through her actions—particularly the importance of not being wasteful despite having abundance.

When I was in my first and second year of high school, I was fortunate that I didn't know what designer clothes were. My mother only bought me two pairs of corduroy pants for the entire school year. One pair was baby blue, and the other was burnt orange. I would alternate each day wearing them, and if someone were paying attention, I'd wear one pair on back-to-back days just to throw them off.

I consider myself extremely lucky to have had a mother who was the way she was when it came to spending money. Some of her examples rubbed off on me.

Whether walking through the house to turn off lights not being used or saving the extra ketchup and napkins from fast-food establishments, seeing my mother do these types of things has helped me save thousands of dollars over the years, both personally and in the restaurant business.

When I was about ten years old, my parents went on a short vacation to Monterrey, Mexico, and left a friend of the family in charge of me and my siblings. For dinner one day, she cooked a large pot of chicken soup. As we were eating it, we all noticed that it had an unusual consistency about it, almost gritty-like. It wasn't until months later that we discovered why.

Early one summer morning, my mother went to the freezer to grab a bag of frozen chicken that she knew was there. She looked and looked for it but couldn't find it anywhere. She was looking for this bag of frozen chicken because she was going to use it as bait for a crabbing trip at a public pier in La Porte. So yes, it turns out that our babysitter made me and my siblings chicken soup using the chicken necks and backs meant for a crabbing trip.

My mother didn't waste anything, including cheap pieces of chicken to go crabbing with. To her, everything had a value until it didn't.

A restaurant must know the cost of every single ingredient it uses to prepare its food, especially the high-cost items like beef, chicken, and seafood. So I stay on the lookout for excessive food waste in our kitchens, especially what is being thrown away. For example, I will look through the trash cans next to a food prep station to see whether or not lettuce is being cored properly. Or I'll go to the three-compartment sink area where we wash dishes to make sure that all of the grated cheese is removed from an empty container.

I also don't like to waste money just because I have it. I heard a quote years ago by former heavyweight boxing champ George Foreman and it stuck in the back of my mind. Foreman said, "Respect every dollar!"[22] I couldn't agree more. Showing respect to every dollar you come into contact with will show that you're disciplined enough to manage more, should you ever get that opportunity.

I tell people all the time that I don't "own" anything; I just get to manage things. And as a matter of fact, I've never liked the word *owner*; to me, it sounds too possessive. I prefer to call myself a manager because that's exactly what I'm doing: I'm managing things. And if I do a good job and I'm responsible with the things

---

22 Timothy L. O'Brien, "Fortune's Fools: Why the Rich Go Broke," *New York Times*, September 17, 2006, https://www.nytimes.com/2006/09/17/business/yourmoney/17broke.html/.

I've been given to manage, I'll be given more things to manage. At some point in the future, I'll have to pass the baton along to someone else and let them manage what I was entrusted with. Hopefully, they'll understand the seriousness of being trusted with such a responsibility.

HOUSEHOLD VERSUS BUSINESS OVERHEAD

A business's overhead plays a major part in whether it will succeed. This is because fixed costs are the same amount each month, and they do not fluctuate with business activity. A business's overhead determines how many sales must be generated to cover expenses. The higher the overhead, the more sales a business must make.

The first and most important overhead a new business must deal with is the owner's lifestyle. Your household overhead will affect every important decision you'll have to make in the business to be successful. If you have too much personal debt, this will only increase the pressure on the business to perform. Sometimes, that alone is the major cause of a business not being able to survive. Not only was the business's overhead difficult to meet, but add to that the cost of an owner's living expenses, and you can see why starting a successful business is difficult.

My income today is substantial, and I have no personal debt. I do use credit cards, but those are paid in full each month. I also have business debt, but I insist on keeping that amount at a conservative level. In my opinion, a strong balance sheet for a restaurant should be one where the debt-to-asset ratio is no higher than 50 percent. Why? Because if a restaurant ends up failing, its assets usually won't be enough to pay off the remaining debt. I've seen many times a restaurant with a stand-alone property, including the land, close down, and when it finally sells, the amount is usually at a fraction of what it costs to build.

No matter what financial position I've found myself in, though, I've strived to keep my spending below my means—to keep my household overhead low. But it sometimes has meant making difficult decisions.

In 1986, after our second child was born, we could no longer afford the house we lived in or the vehicle I was driving. At that time, I was only earning approximately $600 a week. I decided to let my house go into foreclosure, and I returned my 1984 Ford Bronco to the dealership where I had purchased it. Knowing that doing this would ruin my credit, I quickly went out and bought a cheaper vehicle and cut my monthly payment in half. And I was still able to purchase a smaller, more affordable house, which also cut my mortgage payment in half. By better positioning myself financially, I was able to focus on the business at hand, which was to try and make a living in the restaurant business.

In the early 2000s, under much different financial circumstances, Monica and I moved from Pasadena, on the southeast side of Houston, to West University, on the southwest side. We looked for nearly five years before finally finding a house we both liked. This was mainly because we did not see ourselves living in a huge house just for the sake of telling others how many square feet it was. The house had to feel right for us and not anyone else.

When deciding to purchase a high-ticket item like a new home, the most important criterion is to make sure your decision is based solely on your financial means and not with the intention to show another person that you are something other than who you really are. When it comes to spending money, having ulterior motives will always come back and bite you in the behind.

SMART BUSINESS APPROACH

Whenever a new restaurant concept opens up, it takes time to get its footing. There is a lot of evolving that has to happen to build up repeat business.

I have never seen a successful restaurant concept operating the same way as it did when it first opened. Gringo's has been no exception, as we've constantly looked for ways to improve our products and processes over the past thirty years. Even Chick-fil-A isn't the same company today as when it first opened in 1961. Back then, they mainly licensed the chicken sandwich to over fifty eateries, including the Waffle House and the new Houston Astrodome.

Chick-fil-A's founder, Truett Cathy, opened up the first stand-alone unit in 1967 in the food court of the Greenbriar Mall in Atlanta. They looked a lot like a concession stand back then. It wasn't until they built their first freestanding location in 1986 that everything changed, and they've never looked back.

Chick-fil-A revolutionized the drive-through business model, and just about every fast-food chain has borrowed an idea or two from them.

For new restaurateurs, second-generation restaurant buildings are the best types of properties for operating within their means as they get started or start expanding if the size and the layout of the property conform to their concept. For example, in 1999, we purchased a former Red Lobster location in Texas City for $750,000 for our third Gringo's location.

The building consisted of 8,200 square feet and was situated on a two-acre pad with 142 parking spaces. Since most of the restaurant infrastructure (meaning the cooler, freezer, exhaust hood, bar, and grease trap, as well as the kitchen equipment) was already in place, all we had to do was simply "re-skin" the restaurant's interior and exterior. The entire cost to remodel the Texas City location was $450,000. So our total project cost ended up being $1.2 million.

In our first year of operation at this location, we generated over $4 million in sales. That is almost a 4:1 sales-to-investment ratio, which is considered very strong in our industry. Our goal today is a 1:1 ratio, but we're in a much better position financially now, which allows us to purchase real estate and build new Gringo's from the ground up. Once a restaurant brand is established and has a track record of being successful, along with the financials to support it, acquiring funding for new locations becomes a lot easier to secure.

THE DANGER OF LIVING ABOVE YOUR MEANS

Debt and financial mismanagement can affect a person's judgment and moral compass. When I worked at El Toro, I would catch cashiers using their own calculator instead of the cash register to add up the guest check total and then pocket the money. This is referred to in the restaurant industry as *internal shrinkage*, or theft. The temptation to steal for some people is simply too great.

When I opened the first Gringo's thirty years ago, our total budget may have been a total of ten thousand dollars. The only piece of equipment that I bought new was our point-of-sale system. This is the computer system that helps communicate orders from the server to the kitchen and also records and calculates sales. It is a vitally important piece of equipment that restaurants must have to survive, and it makes theft a lot more difficult for staff to get away with.

Let's be honest. It's no fun to be broke and unable to pay your bills. I've been broke before, and it was the worst feeling in the world. A lot of people, despite being broke, still try to live a lifestyle that isn't a true representation of their financial means. They do it because they believe, for one reason or another, that they deserve a certain lifestyle. Or sometimes, the real issue is that they're more concerned about how others see them. I blame a lot of this mindset on social media, where it's become more important to portray a false image of oneself than it is to be who they really are.

Living above one's means may cause some people to do things they wouldn't ordinarily do under different circumstances.

Stealing is bad enough, but ruining your reputation by stealing is something that will have lifelong consequences.

I recommend never spending money you don't have to buy things you don't need to impress people you don't really like. Unfortunately, some people would rather define themselves through the eyes of other people than live a financially stress-free life, which would require them to live below their means.

A POSITIVE IMPACT

Living way below my means over the last thirty years has allowed me not only to increase my net worth but also to continue expanding Gringo's one restaurant at a time. Because I've been financially responsible, I am in a unique position to help others and witness the positive impact it can have on them. I take great joy in being able to help our team members in a time of need. I don't wake up every morning thinking about what I can buy or how much more money I can make. Instead, I think more about whose life I can help change (see Chapter 4).

In helping others, I hope to inspire other individuals with the financial means to do the same. As noted before, Gringo's offers a special Tex-Mex combination plate (Plato Soladado) that benefits the PTSD Foundation of America's Camp Hope, a residential treatment facility in Houston, Texas, that started as an eight-bedroom home providing interim and transitional housing to veterans working to heal their invisible wounds. I reached out to fellow Houston restaurateur Michael Sambrooks to see if he would be interested in supporting Camp Hope in a similar manner. Michael's restaurants include the Pit Room BBQ and the Mexican restaurant Candente.

Michael said that he would definitely give the proposal serious consideration. Six months went by, and I hadn't heard anything back from Michael, so I just figured he either got busy and forgot about it or he had focused on helping other organizations, which I completely understood. Restaurant owners are constantly being asked, almost on a daily basis, to donate food, money, or gift cards.

Then, one morning, I opened up my laptop, and there was an email from Michael. It read:

> Hey Russell,
>
> I wanted to pass along our updated menu with the special for Camp Hope. Apologies, on taking so long to get to this we just did reprints and we over debated the new special for a while.
>
> We have added "La Bandera Plate" to our Tex-Mex Combinations. We just launched the new menu last night and already sold ten plates! I think this should be a pretty successful promotion.
>
> We will send our first donation check at the end of February to Camp Hope.
>
> Sincerely,
> Michael[23]

---

23 Michael Sambrooks, email to the author, February 4, 2023.

I was thrilled Michael had chosen to support Camp Hope. Each of us has the ability to make the world a better place and encourage those around us to do so as well. By living way below your means, you will be able to contribute in ways that can make a difference. Whether you're a small business making a contribution each month to a tremendous organization like Camp Hope or a customer choosing to support an organization through that business's fundraiser, spending your dollars to benefit others is an important way to respect each dollar.

When I finally leave this earth to meet my maker, I want to go knowing that because I chose to live my life well below my means, I had the ability to bless others. But my greatest reward will be knowing that by helping others in need, I inspired other businesses and individuals to do the same.

To-Go Items

1. To live way below your means is spending less than what you earn.

2. When it comes to accumulating wealth, there needs to be a balance between earning money and spending it.

3. Waste is money.

4. The most important overhead a business must deal with is the owner's lifestyle.

5. Debt and financial mismanagement can affect a person's judgment and moral compass.

CHAPTER 10

Live by the Golden Rule

~~~~~~

How do we change the world?
One random act of kindness at a time.

—MORGAN FREEMAN, Twitter post

Whenever I am asked what makes Gringo's so successful, I have to pause before answering. I like to think part of the reason is my business acumen, and of course, I have a talented team that works hard every day to produce quality food and service. But truth be told, our success has more to do with the one particular habit I practice every single day of my life—living by the Golden Rule. Most people probably recognize the Golden Rule as "Do unto others as you would have them do unto you."

I've practiced this habit as far back as I can remember. I've always paid close attention to how people treat others and the response they get when it's done one way, with kindness and empathy, versus the opposite way, with a lack of empathy or concern. I've always noticed that treating other people the exact way I would want to be treated if I found myself in a similar situation will work out to my benefit the majority of the time.

Napoleon Hill, in his book *The Law of Success in Sixteen Lessons*, talks about the Golden Rule in a way that has helped me more fully understand its meaning. Hill writes:

> For more than four thousand years, people have been preaching the Golden Rule as a suitable rule of conduct toward others. But while we have accepted the philosophy of it as a sound rule of ethical conduct, we have failed to understand the spirit of it or the law upon which it is based. The Golden Rule essentially means to do unto others as you would wish others to do unto you if your positions were reversed.[24]

Everyone will reap what they sow. The energy you release toward others will be the exact same energy you'll receive back. If you want to live a peaceful, drama-free, well-balanced life, it would only make sense to purposely and consciously exude the same positivity you want back from those you interact with.

---

24 Napoleon Hill, *The Law of Success in Sixteen Lessons* (Blacksburg, VA: Wilder, 2011), 510.

Hill continues:

> The [Golden Rule] does not stop by merely flinging back upon you your acts of injustice and unkindness toward others; it goes further than this—much further—and returns to you the results of every thought that you release.
>
> Therefore, not only is it advisable to "do unto others as you wish them to do unto you," but to avail yourself fully of the benefits of this great universal law, you must "think of others as you wish them to think of you."[25]

Hill goes on to make the point that the Golden Rule—the one single law that has helped me to achieve a level of success that I had once only dreamed about—begins affecting you either for good or bad the very moment you release a thought.

This is the habit that puts everything together in how to be successful in your life and your business.

FINDING YOUR PURPOSE

I saw a meme on Instagram recently that was an illustration showing two lanes of traffic. The right lane was a right-turn-only

---

25 Hill, *The Law of Success*, 511.

lane with a long line of cars in it. The left lane showed a single car trying to get into the right lane. The caption was a question: Would you let them in?

For me, the answer is very easy. I would definitely let them in, and here's why. I have accidentally found myself in that same situation before. Yes, there will be those who will try to cut into traffic intentionally, but how would you know if it was intentional or simply a mistake? You wouldn't know. There's no way of knowing the other person's true intention. The only thing this scenario should be about is how you would want to be treated if you were ever to find yourself in the same exact circumstances.

I believe we are being tested every day by how we respond to all kinds of situations. If we respond in a selfish way, then that reaction will send us in one direction. If we respond another way, the way we'd want to be treated if we found ourselves in a similar situation, then it's like we just passed an exam and are allowed to graduate and enter the next level of education.

Obviously, a business must generate a profit to survive, but what it does with those profits will always separate it from its competitors. We are able to exhibit the Golden Rule in our company because of the support of our customers. Their patronage allows our business to operate with meaning and purpose. Having purpose motivates me to get up each morning and helps me overlook the trivial things in life and focus on the big things, like helping others, especially our team members.

Years ago, I received a letter from one of our team members at our Texas City location. She shared with me the challenges a fellow team member, Melinda Johnson, was facing and wanted to see if the company could offer any support.

The coworker shared that when Melinda was younger, she had developed cancer and had her leg amputated. Melinda wore a prosthetic, but it was very old—duct taped, super-glued, and broken—and caused her pain and discomfort. Melinda was also a single mother helping her sister get back on her feet, so Melinda couldn't afford to buy a new prosthetic. She worked hard, never complained at work, and never used her disability as a reason not to work as hard or let it bring her down in life. The coworker expressed her wish that she could help Melinda get a new leg but that she knew they were very expensive.

After reading this letter, I felt compelled to do something for Melinda. I contacted John Fernandez, my senior VP of operations, to set up a meeting with Melinda to learn more about her situation. After their meeting, John instructed Melinda to go to her doctor and see what she would need to help her become more independent.

Approximately three weeks later, John sent me the three proposals Melinda had received from her doctor outlining her options. The first option was a base model, which would basically replace what she was already wearing.

The next model up would allow Melinda to walk up the stairs step-over-step and backward. Plus, it would allow her to sit and stand more naturally, as well as cross obstacles more smoothly.

The third model—the Ottobock X3—happened to cost a little over a hundred thousand dollars (or three times more than the base model) and would allow Melinda to work and play around water because it is waterproof. It would also allow her to walk-run-walk and be able to ride a bicycle.

After reviewing the proposals, John and I met to decide which of the three the company would purchase for Melinda. But I also sent John a question I wanted him to ask her once he gave her the news: If money is no object, which model would you choose?

Melinda said she would probably go with the more expensive option because it would allow her to do things like play in the water with her young daughter at the beach without having to remove her prosthetic. It would also allow her to run and ride her bike again, something she had not experienced in years.

As she was explaining why she would choose the more expensive one, Melinda didn't realize we had already decided that if the Ottobock X3 were the one she'd pick if money were no object, then that would be the model Gringo's would purchase for her. John has told me on several occasions that the moment of sharing that news with Melinda was probably the favorite moment of his career.

NO JOB TOO SMALL OR UNIMPORTANT

All jobs, no matter the level, are important to a business's success. So, in keeping with the Golden Rule, it's vital to take care of your employees, especially when they give their all to their work every day, helping ensure the success of your business. And no job is too small or unimportant to receive this care.

Take, for instance, dishwashers in a restaurant. They are a specific breed of worker. They enjoy the solitude that comes with the position yet never seem to complain about the workload. They also have one of the most important positions in the restaurant industry. Can you imagine for a moment what would happen if every dishwasher in the city were to walk out on their job on a Friday night? Restaurants would come to a grinding halt, and I'm positive it would be very challenging to find volunteers willing to jump in and help out.

At Gringo's, the dishwashers work harder than just about anyone else in the restaurant, yet they're invisible to our patrons. The work is monotonous and definitely not glamorous. The dishwasher faces a constant barrage of dirty dishes being dropped off at their workstation from the time we open until we close.

I have a special connection with dishwashers because washing dishes was my first job. Growing up working in my family's restaurant, I would challenge myself to see how fast I could finish a full bus cart of dirty dishes. Back in those days, a busser would push a bus cart through the dining room, clearing off tables of dirty dishes. Once it was full, they would then roll it over to the dishwashing station in the kitchen and change it out for an empty one.

I believe my best time ever was ten minutes to finish a full cart of dirty dishes. The worst part about being a dishwasher, at least for me anyway, was having to wash the pots and pans by hand at the end of the shift. The empty chile con queso pots required a lot of extra elbow grease!

The volume of dishes I washed as a young kid, though, doesn't even come close to the volume of dishes that our dishwashers at Gringo's and Jimmy Changas tackle each and every day. Today, when I visit a Gringo's or Jimmy Changas location, I always make a point to stop by and say hello to and thank the dishwashers on duty.

One of those tireless dishwashers was Abacuc Oliveras, who worked at the Pearland Shadow Creek Gringo's from April 2009 until his passing on July 21, 2013. He was fifty-eight years old.

To most people, Abacuc was simply a dishwasher. To me, he was much more than that. He represented an important part of my company who contributed to the enjoyment of dining out for so many people.

Upon Abacuc's passing, I asked Matt Bussa, general manager at the Pearland Shadow Creek location, what he would remember most about him. He said, "His unbelievable work ethic and picking up his paycheck all dressed up with his cowboy hat and sunglasses on."

While attending his funeral, I witnessed his children weeping over his casket. As I walked over to view his body and pay my respects, I noticed his cowboy hat lying next to him—I almost lost it. Abacuc worked hard, obviously had a loving family, and had the joy of life that comes from those two things.

Do me a small favor. In honor of Abacuc and all the dishwashers who have added to our enjoyment while dining out over the years, the next time you go to a restaurant, consider sending a couple of dollars in an envelope to the dishwashers on duty, along with a note saying, "Thank you! We appreciate you!"

Without a doubt, you will put a huge smile on their face and make them feel as important as they truly are.

HELPING THE COMPETITION

I have wished the absolute best on others, even my competition. I believe competition is what makes all of us better at what we do.

A few years ago, I was reading the *Houston Business Journal* when I came across a story about the Dhanani Group, a very successful Pakistani family from Sugar Land that had just completed the acquisition of a five-unit chain of Mexican restaurants called Cyclone Anayas. I knew very little about this family other than what a mutual friend, J.J. Isbell, had shared with me from time to time. J.J. owns Texas TransEastern, a fuel transport company that delivers fuel to all two hundred gas stations owned by the Dhanani family.

The Dhanani family started in the gas and convenience store business in 1976. Led by the patriarch of the family, Shoukat Shannis, the company has grown into a multibillion-dollar company. It also happens to be one of the largest Burger King, Wendy's, and Popeyes franchisees in America.

When I read the article in the *Houston Business Journal* about the acquisition of Cyclone Anayas, it mentioned that Shoukat's son Usman, a recent MBA graduate from the University of Houston, would be heading up the Mexican restaurant chain. I know how difficult it is to operate a chain of Tex-Mex restaurants, and I knew that this acquisition would be the Dhanani's first attempt at operating a full-service casual concept. So I reached out to them through our friend J.J. and offered to meet and offer any advice I could to help them succeed.

Shoukat, Usman, and another son all agreed to meet with me and my then-COO, Jonathan Kim. We met at Willie G's, a restaurant in the Galleria area of Houston. Jonathan and I were an open book and told them that they were more than welcome to visit any of our restaurants and walk through our kitchens. We offered them a look at anything they needed to help them with this recent acquisition. They were shocked that another Tex-Mex restaurant chain would be willing to share trade secrets with them.

We've since become good friends with the Dhananis, and the Golden Rule played an important role in developing this bond between us. I reached out to them not only because I thought they might be able to use some professional advice from someone with a lot of experience in the Tex-Mex arena but also because I know that if I were to ever find myself in a similar situation of acquiring a concept that was new to me, I would hope that someone, somewhere would reach out and offer me their expertise.

I believe that each of us is in more control of our circumstances than we sometimes realize. It simply requires us just to pause and pay attention to situations that may be happening all around us.

SMALL GESTURES, BIG IMPACT

While attending a University of Houston Cougars basketball game one time, I went to the concession stand to purchase a bottle of water. As I was on my way back to my seat, a man walking in the opposite direction approached me and asked if I was the Master Enchilada Roller. I told him I was.

He introduced himself as John. He went on to say that he and his wife were huge fans of Gringo's and that they used to frequent the original location until they moved to the north side of town and now patronized the New Caney location.

I thanked him and handed John my business card. I told him to email me his mailing address along with his wife's name, and I would have our marketing department mail her a nice gift as our way of saying thank you for the many years of support.

A few days later, I received this email from his wife, Cindy:

> Good Morning, Sir—
>
> Thank you so much for the box of Gringo's gear (and gift card)! What an amazing treat! I am so grateful!
>
> Your kindness and compassion, sir—leave me speechless—
>
> Your generosity to Camp Hope and concern for veterans—
>
> When John and I got married, Beef Marisco was the catered meal of deliciousness. We frequent the New Caney location weekly.

I have sent my appreciation of your loyal employees previously. Santiago, Jasmine, Tyler, Brandon, Miriam (sp)—they are great!

But utmost, sir—the respect you showed my family when Philip Landrum was killed on FM 518. That memory of your employees standing along the procession—absolutely priceless!

I am grateful. I am thankful!

If it had been me who spoke to you at the game, you would have run because I would have cried.

Again, thank you so much, sir!

God's peace and blessings continue for you, sir!

Cindy[26]

I always remind myself that anytime I meet someone in public for the first time, no matter how brief that encounter may be, the impression I leave them with is how they will remember me. I want to make sure I always leave them with a positive one.

What made this encounter at the basketball game that much more remarkable (besides the fact that we catered their wedding reception) was that I had no idea Philip Landrum was one of their family members. Philip had worked under John Fernandez at the Original Gringo's and thrived under John's leadership.

26 Cindy Melby, email to the author, February 23, 2023.

Philip's parents must have seen the positive impact his job had on him because they laid him to rest in his Gringo's uniform.

It goes to show that when you meet someone and treat them with kindness, respect, and generosity, you have the power to make a lasting and genuinely good impression. Through the power of the Golden Rule, you may just be on the receiving end of unexpected connections and opportunities that can aid in your success. Or in my case, I was able to forge even stronger ties with members of our extended Gringo's family.

MY FAVORITE TIME OF THE YEAR

December is always one of my favorite months of the year. It's a great time to reflect on what our company has accomplished over the past eleven months, as well as to continue planning for the future.

One reason I especially enjoy the month of December is because I get to play Santa Claus with my fellow team players. For more than twenty years, our company has been able to give every Gringo's team member a Christmas gift. The value of the gift is dependent on the number of years the individual has worked at our company. Our entire management team really gets excited because December is also the month when we pass out their year-end bonuses.

Besides strong financials, one of the factors I use to determine whether our company is financially stable is the ability to hand out over 2,600 Christmas gifts and year-end bonuses each year. A couple of other factors I like to use are whether or not we're able to pay all of our property taxes before the end of the year, as well as maintain a current status with our vendors.

The reason why these things are so important to me is because operating on a solid financial ground helps us move forward and make the right decisions pertaining to every area of operations. Whether it's making a necessary repair or maintenance decision, continuing to use quality ingredients despite cost increases, giving raises to well-deserving team members, or supporting the community, we are able to do so with a much clearer thought process, knowing that all is well in the financial area of our company.

RANDOM ACTS OF KINDNESS

I once traveled to Mexico City along with my son Derek and his friend to see U2 (my favorite band of all time) perform at Azteca Stadium. On our way back to the States, we arrived at the airport early in the morning and had just cleared security when I decided that the three of us would check into the American Express Centurion lounge.

As I approached the counter, there was a man ahead of us who was having difficulty getting into the lounge. Apparently, his American Express card was one that didn't allow him access. As he was just about to walk away, I quickly asked the young receptionists how many guests I was allowed to bring into the lounge with my Centurion Black Card. She informed me that my card allowed me to bring in up to eight guests.

I quickly told the gentleman that he was my guest and to go ahead into the lounge while I completed my check-in. He began walking very slowly toward the entrance while looking back at me with a very happy yet confused look. He was probably thinking to himself, "Who is this guy, and why did he just do this for me?"

Well, it is very simple. I did it for one reason and one reason only. If I were ever to find myself in a similar situation, I would hope there would be someone who would step up and do the same for me. Anytime I find myself in a situation where I have the opportunity to express a random act of kindness, I will do it. And I'll always do it, never expecting anything in return. The ability to do it is my reward.

We all have opportunities like this every day of our lives. When you take advantage of these opportunities, it will come back to you—unless, of course, you're doing it with the wrong intentions. Practicing the habit of giving and random acts of kindness are just the right things to do. They make you feel good about yourself, and you will live a blessed life as a result.

Another example of how impactful random acts of kindness can be involves two seemingly unconnected things: UPS and paintball.

When my oldest son, Steve, was a teenager, he got into the sport of paintball. The objective of paintball is to fire paint-filled capsules at the opposition, hitting them without being hit yourself and eliminating them from the game. Paintball is relatively safe if players wear eye protection and clothes that cover their bodies.

During one summer, Steve worked at the Johnny Tamales restaurant near our house as a dishwasher, trying to save up enough money to purchase a top-of-the-line paintball gun. Once he was able to save up enough money, he ordered one online. Steve was notified that his paintball gun would be delivered on a Thursday, just in time for a planned weekend outing with his friends to test it out. But when he got home from school on Thursday, there was a yellow UPS sticker on the front door indicating that the driver had attempted to deliver his package but couldn't leave it without getting a signature.

For this not to happen again, Steve asked his mother to stay home on Friday to make sure he received his package. When Steve got home from school on Friday afternoon, however, on the front door was another yellow UPS sticker. It seemed his mother didn't hear the doorbell that afternoon.

When I arrived home from work around five o'clock and learned how disappointed Steve was, I put down my briefcase and said, "Let's go see if we can find your paintball gun."

After trying to locate the delivery truck somewhere near our neighborhood, we went to the UPS distribution center that serviced our area and learned that the package did not originate from there but from another location. But that facility closed at 6:00 p.m., and we only had about twenty minutes to get there. I must have broken every speed limit in an attempt to make it before they closed. When we arrived at the facility, we were able to get inside before they locked the door. Once inside, there was a short line of two customers, so I walked up to the attendant working behind the counter and asked her if the delivery slip originated from this facility. She told us yes, but since the package could be on any number of delivery trucks, there would be no way to retrieve it, and we'd have to wait until Monday to have it delivered.

At that moment, my attempt to make my kid happy was over. As we were about to leave the UPS center, I noticed an elderly couple attempting to ship six large boxes—but they had a dilemma. The cost to ship all these boxes was $165, but the UPS center didn't accept credit cards, which was the only form of payment this couple had on them.

Seeing that they were going to have to load all these boxes back into their vehicle, I decided to see how I could help them out. I approached the counter and told the couple that I'd be more than willing to give them the $165 in cash to ship their boxes. I would just give them my name and address so they could send me a check in the mail. They looked at me like I was from Mars, but they ended up accepting my offer.

The couple did mail me a check for the full amount, along with a very nice card thanking me for the random act of kindness. They turned out to be regulars at the Original Gringo's.

If this story had ended there, I would have been happy knowing I was able to help complete strangers in their time of need, but it didn't—this story got better. The young UPS attendant who told me there was no way of retrieving my son's package was so moved by my helping the couple that she went and found my son's paintball gun, which allowed him to have a wonderful weekend with his friends.

I believe this simple story of wanting to help my son retrieve his paintball gun so he could enjoy it over the weekend illustrates the power of the Golden Rule. The elderly couple attempting to ship multiple boxes wasn't my problem; nor was it really any of my concern. But by putting myself in their shoes, I felt empathy for what they were experiencing.

I didn't offer to loan them the money, thinking that if I did so, it would persuade the UPS worker to retrieve my son's package. It just so happened that the worker noticed, and because of it, she probably was touched by what she had just witnessed. An unexpected, random act of kindness and generosity toward another person is special because it is not very common. It is all the more powerful because it has the ability to persuade and influence other people's actions.

All of us have more control over our lives than we realize; we just have to be aware of what is happening around us. Whenever you do something for another person in need, expecting nothing in return, there is no better feeling in the world.

Everything you do to and for another person, you do to and for yourself.

To-Go Items

1. Whenever you wish the best for others, you wish the best for yourself.

2. What a business does with its profits will always separate it from its competition.

3. Your customers are the reason your business can operate with meaning and purpose.

4. Don't be afraid to help the competition. That kindness will likely be repaid someday.

5. Don't underestimate the power of random acts of kindness.

An Incredible Journey

You can't connect the dots looking forward;
you can only connect them looking backward.

—STEVE JOBS, 2005 Stanford commencement speech

Have you ever visited an amusement park, rode on an exciting new ride, and afterward said to yourself, "I want to do that again!" Up to this point, my life has been pretty much like experiencing your favorite amusement park ride. I have enjoyed it so much that I wish I could do it all over again.

As I connect the dots of my life backward, I can see the influence my parents had on me. And founding Gringo's has given my life meaning and purpose by making our small part of the world, the communities where our restaurants reside, a better place one taco at a time.

January 11, 2024, marked the thirty-first anniversary of Gringo's Tex-Mex. There have been numerous lessons I have learned while on this incredible journey, many of which I detail in this book.

The best part about it? It's not over.

But remember, for all the success that a company achieves, there are always parts of the journey that make that success seem uncertain or unattainable—early failures, financial insecurity, and trouble with personnel. If there is one thing I have always enjoyed observing, though, it is a company that has persevered through the tough times to get to where it is today.

Most successful companies did not start off that way. Gringo's certainly didn't. I keep bringing up the feeling I had when that first car pulled into that empty parking lot over thirty years ago because it signified a new beginning for me—a new chance to build something. It's a feeling I never, ever want to forget.

In 2012, my team and I opened our second Jimmy Changas in League City, Texas. We were scheduled to open at four o'clock, and a line was already forming outside. At least fifty guests were waiting to come inside and give us a try. The time was a quarter till four.

As I was watching our eager customers wait for us to open the doors, I couldn't stand it anymore. I considered these folks to be the most important people in my life, and the last thing I wanted to do was make them wait a minute longer. So, after I checked with my general manager and kitchen manager to see if everything was ready to go, I gave them the green light to open the doors fifteen minutes early.

Remember my formula for success? Positive values = Positive habits = Success. When you determine what values you want to live your life around and the core values of your business, simply develop positive habits around those to live by each day. Here are a few more success habits of the Master Enchilada Roller that may be helpful to you:

1. *Life doesn't have to be complicated.* Remember to do what you value and value what you do. Only you can determine what is truly important in life. There are simple rules for life and business. Success is simple, just not easy.

2. *Always remember to think before you speak.* Imagine all the conversations you have each day with family, business associates, team members, vendors, and customers and the regular interactions with people in your community and circle of influence. It takes just one comment that is taken the wrong way to send the wrong signal. Words are important. Before you speak, make sure to think about how you want that other person to feel. As the adage goes, people may not remember what you said, but they will always remember how you made them feel.

3. *Associate only with positive individuals.* Business philosopher and author Jim Rohn said that you're the average of the five people you hang around the most.[27] Over the

---

27 Connie Stemmle, "You Are the Average of the Five People Quote: 5 Lessons," *Develop Good Habits*, August 30, 2023, https://www.developgoodhabits.com/five-people/.

last six decades of my life, I have seen how much influence the people around me can have. I have chosen to put positive people around me so I will be influenced in the right direction. The people closest to you definitely influence your thinking and, therefore, your actions more than you may realize. And, if I may, let me also include the media in the mix. Whatever you put in your mind through your eyes or ears will slowly but surely change you. Are you sure you're listening to the truth? Personal development pioneer Earl Nightingale said, "Whatever you plant in your subconscious mind and nourish with repetition and emotion will eventually become a reality."[28] Will what you are watching and listening to today take you where you want to go tomorrow?

4. *Approach all of life with a win-win attitude.* Speaking of media and what we watch and listen to, the world at large seems to think that in every transaction, there is a win-lose scenario. It doesn't have to be that way. When you add value to everyone you know, everyone wins. When you offer a quality product for the lowest price possible, you win, and the customer wins. When you practice conscious capitalism, you give back to your team, the community, and the needs of our world—everyone wins. Are you a go-getter or a go-giver?

---

28 Peter Economy, "37 Earl Nightingale Quotes That Will Empower You to Soar High," *Inc.*, October 2, 2015, https://www.inc.com/peter-economy/37-earl-nightingale-quotes-that-will-empower-you-to-soar-high.html/.

We came into this world with nothing, and we will leave with nothing. Inheritance is something you leave *to* someone, but legacy is what you leave *in* someone. The latter is the most important thing and the thing that will define you for eternity.

Six months before Dr. Martin Luther King Jr. was assassinated, he spoke to a group of junior high students outside Philadelphia. He used the analogy of how just like a building needs a blueprint to be well constructed, so too do people need a blueprint for their lives. He suggested that one of the things that must be in a person's blueprint is a deep belief in their own dignity, worth, and *somebody-ness*. The second thing Dr. King said must be on this blueprint was the determination to achieve excellence in their fields of endeavor. Dr. King finished his speech by telling the students that no matter what they end up becoming in life, they should do it to the best of their ability.

Today, whenever I am asked by someone what line of work I'm in, I proudly say, "I serve tacos and enchiladas for a living." I have gotten way past the trap of defining myself through the eyes of other people. How someone views me today is way less important than it once was, and that is because now my primary focus in life and in business is simply to be the very best that I can be by surrounding myself with people who help make me a better person and by first believing in myself.

I hope that sharing my life, my values, and my habits will help you be not only more successful but also, more importantly, more significant.

I'd like to finish this book by sharing one of my favorite

episodes of *The Jeffersons*. For those who are too young to remember, *The Jeffersons* was a sitcom that ran from 1975 to 1985 about a successful African American businessman who ran a chain of dry cleaners throughout New York City. You may remember the theme song, "Movin' On Up."

In this particular episode, Mr. Jefferson is visiting one of his locations when an elderly customer comes in to pick up her dry cleaning. She fumbles through her purse, looking for money, and then admits she doesn't have the payment right now. Mr. Jefferson tells her not to worry about it—he'll put it on her account. After she leaves, he just tears up the bill. The woman, as the episode reveals earlier, had been his very first customer years before and had given him his first dollar. Mr. Jefferson never forgot that support.

Being in business is about much more than just making money. It is about using that business as a *vehicle* to make a positive impact on those it comes into contact with.

From the customers to the employees and from the vendors to the community, everyone benefits when a business realizes that its success is best when shared. I'm grateful that our company has been able to share its success with our community. That has been my greatest reward.

Follow me on Instagram for more success habits.

If you ever get the opportunity to dine at one of our restaurants, please feel free to email me directly at book@gringostexmex.com.

Afterword

I had the pleasure of compiling the wonderful stories, lessons, and habits you just read. I asked Russell if I could share how this book came about and my experience of getting to know Russell and putting his writings into this book. Obviously, he agreed.

Before I met Russell, the only thing I knew about Gringo's was that it was a Mexican restaurant near my office in Stafford, Texas, where On the Border was previously located. Since I'm not in the restaurant business, I never thought about who owned it.

I first met Russell at a party at the home of radio personality Michael Berry. About seventy people, including my wife and me, were gathered there to get to know each other before going on a VIP group trip we would all be taking in about two weeks.

The trip was with supporters and fans of Michael's radio show, of which my wife is a superfan, to say the least. She listens to him *all day long.* My wife, Denise, is a bona fide legend in the radio industry. She has sold more radio advertising in the great state of Texas than any other single human being in history! Before she retired, she was inducted into the Texas Radio Hall of Fame. She knew Michael before he became the Czar of Talk Radio.

The trip was to West Palm Beach. When Denise told me she wanted to go on it, I asked her how much it was. "Twenty-five thousand dollars per couple."

"Twenty-five thousand dollars to go to West Palm Beach with a bunch of people I don't even know?" I pressed. "Why would I spend that kind of money to go to West Palm Beach with others when we could go by ourselves for much less? Besides, I don't need to fly on a private jet."

I really didn't want to go, but Denise has always supported my dreams and has always been diligent, faithful, and hard-working. She has never denied me anything, and so I agreed to go. Plus, we are very blessed financially and debt-free, so the money was not an issue. I messaged my office and told them to cut the check.

At the party, we met Lee Majors (the Six Million Dollar Man), who is one of my childhood TV heroes, as well as Dan Pastorini, a former quarterback of the Houston Oilers during the Luv Ya Blue days. Little did I know that a man by the name of Russell Ybarra would become a significant connection. We were mingling on the sprawling patio, lit by hanging lights like you might see in an outdoor seating area at a restaurant. Drinks were being served, and someone was frying catfish. It seems like there was a story behind the catfish, but I don't remember what it was.

What I do remember vividly was that the background music stopped, and Michael Berry took to the porch, which was slightly higher than the patio, with microphone in hand. He thanked everyone for participating and shared that the proceeds of the trip would be donated to Camp Hope. He thanked the celebrities for coming out and those of us who were going on the trip. What he said next floored me. "And I would like to thank Russell for sponsoring four couples on this trip who ordinarily would not be able to afford to go."

It doesn't take long to do that math. Four times $25,000. You got it—*$100,000!* I looked over to see an unassuming man with a bit of a bashful grin on his face, standing next to a petite, beautiful woman who was dressed perfectly for the occasion and obviously sweet and humble as well. You could just tell that. Anyone could immediately tell this was a special couple. It was right there and then that I began to learn about the heart of Russell Ybarra. Later on, I would learn about his love for his team, his passion for excellence, and his huge respect for our military.

To get to know the others on the trip, my wife and I packaged up three of my books in a little colored gift bag that we gave to each couple as they left the party. I have a business coaching and training company, and I figured that many of the couples were probably business owners or had some connection to the business world. I felt it would be a nice gesture to give my fellow travelers a gift, and it would at least plant a seed of service and, who knows, maybe lead to a significant connection.

Once on the trip, I found myself in a buffet line behind Russell. I had briefly chatted with him and Monica at the pre-trip party. It was at this time that I learned that not only was he the founder and owner of Gringo's, but he also employed more than 2,500 team members (and that his wife had recently become a client of another business I own). We spent a few minutes chatting as the line shifted forward. His next statement truly caught me by surprise.

"I should have you ghostwrite my book."

"Ghostwrite your *book*?" I returned.

"Well, I'm sixty years old, and I think it's time to get my story on paper."

I was surprised by the statement, and the immediate environment was obviously not the place to have a meaningful conversation, so I said, "Great. Let's talk about it while we are on the trip." Mostly, I needed some space and time to think about his comment because I'm an author, not a ghostwriter.

Also, Russell is a quiet man, and I wasn't sure exactly how to approach him. My nature is outgoing, gregarious, and sometimes downright silly, so I didn't press. But I was definitely intrigued. Knowing what I knew about Russell by now, I certainly didn't want to do anything goofy that might cause him concern. The opportunity for another conversation presented itself near the pool at the hotel overlooking the beach.

"Would you like to tell me more about this book you want to write?" I began. "Why do you want to write a book?"

He told me that he wanted to put down his story for his

grandkids so they would really know who he was as a person. And he wanted to use the proceeds to support Camp Hope. I thought to myself, "Those are two great reasons to write a book." But I wondered out loud, "Why me?"

He explained to me that he had read one of the books I gave out at the party. Actually, I think he had listened to the audio-book. Other people began to arrive, so I ended the conversation with, "Great. Let's set up a call after the trip."

A couple of weeks later, I was on the phone with Russell. I began our conversation with, "*If* I'm the right person to do this . . ."

Russell stopped me mid-sentence and said, "Oh, you're the right person."

"Why do you feel that way?" I inquired.

"You and I have the exact same values," he explained. I was still questioning whether I should take this opportunity because I'm not a ghostwriter. However, I have published twelve books of my own, which include a compilation book called *Phenomenal Success Stories*, in which several of my coaching clients' success stories appear. I also had a coauthor on one of my books. Plus, I've self-published on Amazon, I've used three smaller publishers, and *The Power of Community* was published by one of the largest publishing companies in the world.

And, of course, I have worked closely with some of the top business authors in America, including Zig Ziglar, John C. Maxwell, and Michael Gerber. One of my closest associates owns a publishing company, and I coach many of her authors. So I knew I could do it. I just had never done it, so I wasn't completely sold on the idea. But this is Russell Ybarra! Plus, I learned that he already had lots of content to work with.

To be clear, I did not ghostwrite this book. All of this book was written by Russell himself. I just compiled the wonderful stories, habits, and lessons here. My job was to sift through all the content, rearrange it, revise it, and put it in the best format. It was a slow, painstaking process. There is nothing easy about writing a book, compiling content, or editing the content once developed.

Even when you have finished the draft, you still haven't even gotten started! Then comes the publishing process, getting critical feedback and endorsements, and potentially rewriting or updating the content again. Even *then*, you haven't really started! Next comes the printing, marketing, and everything else that happens before the book gets into the hands of the reader.

But the effort was worth it. I was touched as I read through the stories, lessons, and habits. I feel honored to have spent the past few months in this great man's mind. He has a heart of gold. He is humble, hungry, and smart.

One of my early meetings with Russell was at his corporate office in La Porte, Texas. As we walked around, we visited each of the executive team members in their office. At that point, I had not been immersed in the content yet, so I was trying to get a feel for how his team members saw him.

"What's the most important thing you appreciate about Russell?" I asked each of them. Before they could respond, Russell quickly ducked out of their office and closed the door behind him. He is so humble that he either didn't want to influence the answer, allow anything to go to his head, or both. I heard over and over again, "He's such a giver," "He has a huge heart," or "He loves every person here." One person even said, "That man is the most amazing human being I've ever known."

I heard the same thing when I visited some of the Gringo's restaurants and chatted with the managers, many of whom have been there for decades. I'm sure you've gotten that sense as you read through this book. And we haven't even scratched the surface yet. These are only a handful of stories over a thirty-year period in business and an extraordinary *six decades* on the planet. Phenomenal business success is truly about values. Your values determine your habits, and your habits create the success you have. But it starts with principles. It starts with values. It starts with the heart. When you get your heart right, you can get your head right. And when you get your head right, your hands will follow, and you will plant the *seeds of service* that Russell talks about.

I think I really began to understand Russell's heart when we were having lunch one day. It's interesting to have lunch with someone who is such an accomplished restaurateur. I was filing through the manilla folder with the pages I had compiled for Russell. I glanced at the tortilla chips on the table and wondered what he tasted when he ate someone else's chip. I wondered what he thought about the service and the decor. But we had other business to take care of, so we began talking about his philosophy of life.

One of the other honors I've been graced with is to help carry on the legacy of Zig Ziglar. His famous quote (and his favorite until the day he passed away) is, "You will get all you want in life, if you help enough other people get what they want."[29] I believe that. I have seen the evidence of that. However, when I quoted it during our lunch conversation, Russell shot back, "Unless that's the reason you're doing it." *Mic drop!*

You see, planting seeds of service with the wrong motive may get you results, but not the kind you want. Doing things for others solely to benefit yourself robs you of the joy, the peace, and the satisfaction you really want. It has to be genuine. It has to be real. I can say without hesitation that Russell doesn't give to get. It's just who he is. And you can be that person, too.

All you have to do is adopt the values in this book and live by them every day.

HOWARD PARTRIDGE
Best-selling author, business owner,
and international business coach

---

29 Kevin Kruse, "Zig Ziglar: 10 Quotes That Can Change Your Life," *Forbes*, November 28, 2012, https://www.forbes.com/sites/kevinkruse/2012/11/28/zig-ziglar-10-quotes-that-can-change-your-life/?sh=38089d3b26a0/.

Acknowledgments

~~~~~~

This book would not have been written without the support of so many wonderful people, starting with Howard Partridge and my COO, Heather McKeon, both of whom held my hand to help get the book over the finish line.

There have been many others who've played a major part in my life, and I list them with the hope that I have not left anyone out. If I have forgotten anyone, I hope they accept my apologies and know that I'm eternally grateful to them.

I have to start with my dad, Eugene Ybarra, for giving me my first job as a dishwasher, and my mother, Alice, for raising me and all my siblings, Tony, Victor, Erick, Alice, Moses, Roland, and Troy. I love them all very much.

I thank Jesse Garcia for seeing something in me before I did; Larry Forehand for giving me a shot at selling him tortillas in the 1980s; architect Davis Wilson, who held my hand to help me build my first restaurant from the ground up; David Tai, Don Wang, and Carlos Alvarez with MetroBank for loaning me the money to build the second Gringo's in La Porte in 1996; Craig Schuster for coming up with some incredible design ideas; general contractors Kevin Thomas and Bert Harvey; and interior designers Deborah Goolsby and Stephanie Fernandez.

Gringo's wouldn't be the company it is today without my executive and operations team members and the rest of our corporate support team members: Jonathan Kim, Heather McKeon, Danny Hanks, Joe Ivey, Elio Alfonso, Al Flores, John Fernandez, Matt Bussa, Kevin Carroll, Sam Hernandez, George Tannous, Justin Saunders, Hugo Olvera, Alex Chicas, Nico Rodriguez, Andy Roach, Chuck Rivera, Kelly Ivie, Chrissy Henson, Joey Farina, and Lindi Stripling.

And last but certainly not least, I thank my wife, Monica, for all her love and support, and our two sons, Steve and Derek, and their wives, Hilary and Skylar, for giving our family the most beautiful gifts I could've ever dreamed of: our grandchildren, Wyatt, Jonah, Eleanor, Claire, and Daphne Moon.

About the Author

RUSSELL YBARRA (a.k.a. the Master Enchilada Roller) owns one of the most exciting Tex-Mex chains in the country, with 2,600 team members and twenty-four locations (and continuing to expand).

Despite his beginnings as a C student at best, Russell has become not only a successful business owner, with revenues pushing $160 million per year, but also a beloved leader and one of the most faithful givers you will ever meet.

Russell is also extremely grateful for the men and women who have served our country, which allows the rest of us to live in peace. Therefore, all profits from this book are donated to the PTSD Foundation of America's Camp Hope, a peer-to-peer residential program for veterans, providing hope and healing from the unseen wounds of war.

Combat Trauma Helpline: 877-717-PTSD (7873)

Follow Russell on Instagram: @russellybarra

Have comments about the book? Email book@gringostexmex.com.